THE FULL MONTY

THE FULL MONTY

BOOK BY TERRENCE MCNALLY

MUSIC & LYRICS BY DAVID YAZBEK

BASED ON THE MOTION PICTURE RELEASED BY FOX SEARCHLIGHT PICTURES
AND WRITTEN BY SIMON BEAUFOY, PRODUCED BY UBERTO PASOLINI
AND DIRECTED BY PETER CATTANEO

APPLAUSE
THEATRE & CINEMA BOOKS

The Full Monty
Book by Terrence McNally
Music and Lyrics by David Yazbek
Based on the Motion Picture released by Fox Searchlight Pictures and written by Simon Beaufoy,
produced by Uberto Pasolini and directed by Peter Cattaneo

Copyright © 2002 by Terrence McNally and Yeidlesounds Co., LLC (BMI)
Libretto Copyright © 2002 by Terrence McNally
Lyrics Copyright © 2000, 2002 by Yeidlesounds Co., LLC (BMI)
Foreword Copyright © 2002 by Jack O'Brien
All Rights Reserved.

Photos by Carol Rosegg and Craig Schwartz, courtesy Barlow Hartman Public Relations, 1560 Broadway, Suite 909, New York, NY 10036

ISBN: 0-7394-2869-1   Printed in Canada

Applause Theatre & Cinema Books
151 West 46th Street, 8th Floor
New York, NY 10036
Phone: (212) 575-9265
Fax: (646) 562-5852
Email: info@applausepub.com
Internet: www.applausepub.com

Piano/vocal/guitar selections from *The Full Monty* also available from Hal Leonard Corporation:
www.halleonard.com
Inventory #HL00313168

SALES & DISTRIBUTION

North America:
HAL LEONARD CORP.
7777 West Bluemound Road
P. O. Box 13819
Milwaukee, WI 53213
Phone: (414) 774-3630
Fax: (414) 774-3259
Email: halinfo@halleonard.com
Internet: www.halleonard.com

UK:
Combined Book Services LTD.
Units I/K, Paddock Wood Distribution Centre
Paddock Wood, Tonbridge, Kent TN12 6UU
Phone: (44) 01892 837171
Fax: (44) 01892 837272
United Kingdom

Produced on Broadway by
Fox Searchlight Pictures, Lindsay Law, Thomas Hall
World Premiere at the
Old Globe Theatre, San Diego, California.

STRIPPING THE WILD, FULL MONTY

How does a musical theatre piece actually "happen" these days? One has long reflected on elegant memories of Noël Coward, wrapped smugly in his smoking jacket, champagne flute in hand, while appropriating the piano in the bar of a first-class hotel in Singapore, or wistfully conjured up the image of Cole Porter and Moss Hart hilariously tossing back identical gin fizzes on some high sea or another while *Jubilee* wafted gently into soft focus somewhere "over there." Whatever happened to those methods? Did the license for careless, creative fun utterly expire midway through the last century in the face of rising costs and union headaches?

Well, perhaps not entirely. For in the Spring of 1998 the phone in my office in the Globe Theatres in San Diego rang and on the other end was my great and good friend, Lindsay Law, then president of Fox Searchlight Pictures in Los Angeles. Lindsay and I had been close associates since 1975 when he was a young producer taking over a dropped Great Performances television opportunity that John Houseman's Acting Company was only too happy to oblige by fulfilling. It happened that my production of Saroyan's *The Time of Your Life* was the candidate for that television transference, and the result was a lifetime of close friendship with Lindsay, who subsequently piloted me through television versions of things as disparate as Arthur Miller's *All My Sons* and a live TV broadcast of Thornton Wilder's *The Skin of Our Teeth* for his American Playhouse from the very stage of the theatre just below my office. We had even shared digs over the years when we were broke, and had vacationed in Mexico when we had the time, but since Lindsay had taken the creative reins at Fox Searchlight, we hadn't seen all that much of each other. His string of hits at that studio was truly astonishing, but perhaps nothing was quite as flashy, as remarkable, and as successful as *The Full Monty*, the "little film that could," which became the highest grossing independent film of the year, earning Oscar nominations and going into various record books on both sides of the Atlantic.

What I was yet to understand was that this meteoric little hit had been attracting the interest of theatre producers like nothing since the unclothed Vilma Banky hit Hollywood, and Lindsay had been fending off various offers to turn the film into a musical from writers, lyricists, composers, and, for all I knew, stage hands.

"What do you think of *The Full Monty* as a musical?" was his fairly abrupt and dry opening. That's all I remember hearing, and that, as the expression has it, is how I met your Grandmother!

I've always believed that certain productions either "want" to happen, or they don't, and if a project is lucky enough to be one of the former, from the opening gun there is nearly nothing you can do to stop it.

Monty was one of those. Having worked with me as director before, and having seen what my Managing Director/partner Tom Hall and the Globe itself could do with, for instance, that live shoot of *Skin*, Lindsay had a clear methodology in mind which exactly matched my own: we could easily put the musical into a season here in San Diego, have a controlled environment in which to explore and perfect the project away from public scrutiny, and with Fox putting up all the money, and the Globe supplying the "talent," we could not only do the show fairly simply, but quickly.

Several things were apparent from the get-go: my business partner, Tom Hall, a savvy, experienced professional, beautifully matched Lindsay's overview with a skill set that brought nuts and bolts theatrical practicality to the table. He was looking for the best way to make a transition out of his present position, and an alliance with Lindsay and *Monty* would be the perfect opportunity. That was the first given. The second was our unanimous choice of much-decorated playwright Terrence McNally to write the book. Terrence, too, had been a collaborator of mine ten years earlier, once again at the Globe, and we had been looking longingly for some project that would put us together creatively ever since. When I called Terrence in New York, his immediate reaction was "I would have been furious if you *hadn't* asked me!" And the final key figure to add to the ready-made mix was choreographer Jerry Mitchell, a wildly enthusiastic and gifted collaborator I'd solicited for several other opportunities, but timing had always been against us. Among his most celebrated achievements had been the institution of "Broadway Bares," a brilliant annual fund-raiser for AIDS support for which the Broadway performing community comes together and literally strips for money. No one in the business knows more about taking clothes off in public than Jerry Mitchell!

But who would write the score? The first thing we asked ourselves was whose music was suggested by the conception of *The Full Monty*, and we came up fairly empty handed; although the musical field is ripe with genuine and varied talent, none of the recognizable names seemed to ring quite the bell of recognition one would hope. As it happened, the Globe was at that time mounting a new production of the Adam Guettel/Tina Landau musical *Floyd Collins*, and it occurred to me that one of the newer, younger composers working in the industry might be a likely collaborator. I asked Adam if he himself might be interested, but he was already committed to another project, and responsibly stepped away from the offer. But in doing so, mentioned one of his closest friends, a composer named David Yazbek who had never before written a show, but whose witty and off-beat CDs were already beginning to generate a great deal of interest. And Adam said one thing to me that made the whole thing click. He said "He knows the 'hook' of a song, and his work has edge!" That sounded like our man.

David's immediate reaction was positive. He had a few brief meetings with Terrence to see if their collaborative skills might mesh, and swiftly supplied us with three or four songs, two of which are in the current score.

Adding musical director Ted Sperling and orchestrator Harold Wheeler to the roster, and choosing John Arnone and Howell Binkley as our set and lighting designers, and, for costumes, Robert Morgan, one of the Globe family of Associate Artists, we were finally off and running.

And "running" was the keyword, because harkening back to those halcyon days when a creative team like Rodgers and Hart or the Gershwins got an idea, and the very next season that idea was playing the Music Box, we determined to get the show on for the very next season, opening late in the spring at the Globe, and bringing the show to Broadway in that same fall.

But how do I speak of the fun that ensued? As Tolstoy renders all happy families as happy in the same way, perhaps collaborations follow along. There were difficult moments, yes, moments of query and even consternation, but mostly we had a truly glorious time. Chemistry in casting, we all know full well, is over 80% of the director's job. But it's no less true of creating a show as well. If the components come together with grace, good will and joy, and with genuine enthusiasm and respect for each other's work, the piece fairly delivers itself. And on June 1, 2000, at the Globe in San Diego, California, and subsequently on the night of October 26th, *The Full Monty* stood up as a bona fide, original, human, funny and touching American musical, which wowed its audiences on both coasts, and now, as I write this, has gone on to play across the nation as well, in Barcelona, in Rome, and in the famed West End of London.

The journey of out-of-work steel workers from Sheffield, England to Buffalo, New York isn't as odd, or even as far out as one might suppose. The remarkable spark that makes people finally get off their dead duffs and do something with their lives is a universal one, and the rocket that is *The Full Monty* has a trajectory into the theatrical heavens that delivers a very special brand of those fireworks, indeed.

I'm sure I speak for all the collaborators involved, the actors, and the various staffs that have served it when I say of this experience: I wouldn't have missed it for the world!

Jack O'Brien, Director
San Diego, California

The Full Monty premiered at the Old Globe Theatre in San Diego, California, on June 1, 2000. Its Broadway premiere was at the Eugene O'Neill Theatre on October 26, 2000. It was produced by Fox Searchlight Pictures Inc., Lindsay Law, and Thomas Hall. It was directed by Jack O'Brien and choreographed by Jerry Mitchell. The set designs were by John Arnone, the costume designs were by Robert Morgan, the lighting design was by Howell Binkley, and the sound design was by Tom Clark. The composer and lyricist was David Yazbek, the music director and vocal and incidental music arrangements were by Ted Sperling, the orchestrations were by Harold Wheeler, dance music arrangements by Zane Mark, and the show was conducted by Kimberly Grigsby. The production supervisor was Gene O'Donovan and the production stage manager was Nancy Harrington. Casting was by Liz Woodman Casting. The book was written by Terrence McNally, based on the motion picture released by Fox Searchlight Pictures and written by Simon Beaufoy, produced by Uberto Pasolini and directed by Peter Cattaneo. Press representative was Barlow-Hartman Public Relations and general management was provided by The Charlotte Wilcox Company.

THE CAST
(IN ORDER OF APPEARANCE)

Georgie Bukatinsky	Annie Golden
Buddy "Keno" Walsh	Denis Jones
Reg Willoughby	Todd Weeks
Jerry Lukowski	Patrick Wilson
Dave Bukatinsky	John Ellison Conlee
Malcolm MacGregor	Jason Danieley
Ethan Girard	Romain Frugé
Nathan Lukowski	Nicholas Cutro or Thomas M. Fiss
Susan Hershey	Laura Marie Duncan
Joanie Lish	Jannie Jones
Estelle Genovese	Liz McConahay
Pam Lukowski	Lisa Datz
Teddy Slaughter	Angelo Fraboni
Molly MacGregor	Patti Perkins
Harold Nichols	Marcus Neville
Vicki Nichols	Emily Skinner
Jeanette Burmeister	Kathleen Freeman
Noah "Horse" T. Simmons	André De Shields
Police Sergeant	C.E. Smith
Minister	Jay Douglas
Tony Giordano	Jimmy Smagula

The Players

Jerry Lukowski, an unemployed mill worker
Nathan Lukowski, his young son

Pam Lukowski, his estranged wife
Teddy Slaughter, her live-in boyfriend

Dave Bukatinsky, an unemployed mill worker
Georgie Bukatinsky, his wife

Harold Nichols, an unemployed supervisor at the same mill
Vicki Nichols, his wife

Malcolm MacGregor, an unemployed mill worker
Molly MacGregor, his ailing mother

Ethan Girard, an unemployed mill worker

Noah (Horse) T. Simmons, a retired mill worker

Jeanette A. Burmeister, a piano player of indeterminate years

Buddy (Keno) Walsh, a male stripper

Reg Willoughby, an unemployed mill worker
Tony Giordano, a Buffalo club owner

Estelle Genovese, Jerry's occasional girlfriend
Susan Hershey, a friend of Pam and Georgie's
Joanie Lish, another friend of Pam and Georgie's

The Setting

Buffalo, New York

The Time

The Present

THE FULL MONTY

ACT ONE

There is a drum roll and a cymbal crash.

The lights come up on a small, raised platform. A spotlight defines a tight, bright circle of white light on it.

A young woman bounds onto the platform. She wears jeans and a sweater. She holds a hand mike in one hand. Her name is GEORGIE BUKATINSKY.

GEORGIE
Welcome to Girls' Night Out. Who says Buffalo doesn't rock?

(*Big cheers*)

Hi, I'm Georgie Bukatinsky from the Florsheim Outlet at the Miracle Mall over on Route 11. Let's hear it for gals who work!

(*Big cheers*)

I told my husband, Davie (he's home doing the dishes) I said, "Big man, gals who work are gals who like to play!" Was I right?

(*Big cheers*)

All right, let's play!

(*Music. A special light comes on. Standing in it is BUDDY (KENO) WALSH.*

Right now BUDDY appears to be more an icon than a real person. He is the perfect, well-heeled businessman in an expensive suit carrying an expensive attaché case)

His name is Buddy (Keno) Walsh. He's all the way from the Big Apple.

(*Cheerful boos for New York City*)

New York ain't so bad, as long as you don't have to live there!

(*Anti-NYC jokes go over big in* GEORGIE'S *part of the world*)

(*The band begins a sexy vamp.* BUDDY *starts to move to it.*

BUDDY *removes his jacket. Pandemonium.*

He turns around and bends over, giving his audience a good view of his rear-end. Delirium)

I told Mr. Walsh we were going to behave ourselves. So I lied! He's all yours!

(*She runs off, leaving* BUDDY *center stage to continue his dance. His dance soon has the women screaming.*

A WOMAN *has run up to the platform and stuffed a dollar in* BUDDY'S *waistband!*)

GEORGIE
You're kind of jumping the gun, honey.

(*New pandemonium. The* WOMAN *puts her face in her hands ("I can't believe what I've done!") and runs off, leaving* BUDDY *center stage to continue his dance. Pretty soon he is down to his G-string and we get a nice view of his rear end as he exits. The* WOMEN *cheer wildly.* GEORGIE *steps forward*)

GEORGIE
Buddy "Keno" Walsh, ladies! Don't worry, ladies, there's plenty more where that came from. We know what you want and we're gonna give it to you.

(*The lights are fading on* GEORGIE)

TRANSITION

> (*Lights come up on* **REG WILLOUGHBY**, *a union leader. He is facing an angry group of unemployed mill workers*)

REG
All right, all right! Quiet down! One at a time!

GARY BONASORTE
When they closed the plant it's like they threw us out with the garbage.

MARTY
I've been out of a job eighteen months. I got a mortgage and four kids.

REG
Your union hears you, gentlemen!

JERRY
What is our union *doing* about us?

REG
Everything we can to get you back to work.

JERRY
I got a kid out there. What am I supposed to tell him? That I used to be a foreman?

DAVE
You were a great foreman.

JERRY
Tell that to Nath. Tell him there used to be a mill. He likes a good story.

> (*This young man's name is* **JERRY LUKOWSKI**)

DAVE
Don't get started, Jerry.

(*JERRY'S* best friend is *DAVE BUKATINSKY*)

REG
That's the sort of attitude that will get you nowhere. I've got your checks. When I call your name, raise your hand. Lukowski, Jerry.

(*JERRY doesn't want to raise his hand*)

Lukowski, Jerry.

(*He caves. REG hands him his weekly dole*)

REG
Instead of grousing about what your union is gonna do for you, think about what you can do for yourself. That goes for all of you. What do *you* want? Bonasorte, Gary.

(*He starts handing out the other checks*)

SONG: SCRAP

JERRY
What I want? That's easy, asshole — I want a job.
I want to feel like a person instead of a slob.
I want to wake up knowing where I'm gonna go.
Not going nowhere, wandering the streets of Buffalo
'Cause it's a slow town,
When you don't know where to go.

I'll be wetting down the razor, then I'll figure
"What's the point?" so I go into the living room,
Roll another joint, then lunch, then a beer,
Then sitting like an an ape on the sofa with a hanky
And the same old porno tape.

And that's a big day when you're scrap.

DAVE

What I want? I'll tell you Jerky — I want a life.
I want to feel like the husband instead of the wife.
I want to get some sleep when I go to bed
'Stead of lying there digging through
The garbage in my head.

JERRY & DAVE

And it's a long night when you're scrap.
It's a long, long night when you're scrap.

MALCOLM

I know what I want. A place of my own. It could be a room even.
Just so it's mine.

ETHAN

I still don't know what I want. Something. Somebody.

I guess I'm lonely.

MALCOLM

I'm lonely.
I don't know what to do.
I should get out.

ETHAN

A bar,

ETHAN & MALCOLM

A party or two.

MALCOLM

I sure could use a friend.

ETHAN

Somebody,

ETHAN & MALCOLM

Somebody new.

ETHAN & MALCOLM
But there's that horrifying moment when they ask you what you do.

MALCOLM
Hi. I'm Malcolm, a complete loser who still lives at home with his mother.

DAVE
Hi, I'm Dave Bukatinsky. I just defrosted my refrigerator and vac-uumed my living room. And how was your day?

JERRY
Hi, I'm Jerry Lukowski. I'm thiry-two, out of work, divorced, in debt up to my balls, I need some serious dental work, if I don't make some money soon, they won't let me see my kid, I'm fed up, frustrated, angry, and, oh yeah...

ALL MEN	
Scrap!	**REG**
	That's it for tonight.
Scrap!	
	See you next week.
Scrap!	
	Let's clean up.

MEN
So what I want — that's easy —
I want to understand,
How I got to be a loser
And I used to be a man.
And I don't know where I'm going
And I don't know why I'm here
All I know is that the future
Will include another beer.

MALCOLM
And that's important —

             JERRY & OTHERS
             And that's important —

                          DAVE & OTHERS
                          And that's important —

ETHAN & OTHERS
And that's important —

DAVE, & OTHERS
I just want some veal
Or a steak on the table.
'S that too much to ask?

                          ETHAN & OTHERS
                          I just want

             JERRY, MALCOLM   *Something real,*
                  & OTHERS   *Something right,*
             I just want   *Something stable.*
             To feel like   *'S that too much*
             I know what   *To ask?*
             My label is.
             Just tell me what
             My label is.

Just give me anything   *I'm happy to be*   *Just give me*
I don't wanna be...   *Anything but...*   *Anything but...*

                    MEN
Scrap. Scrap.
Scrap. Scrap.
Scrap. Scrap.

Scra-yea-yea-yea-yea-yea-yea-yea-yea-yea-p!

> (*Outside Tony Giordano's club. We can hear the music playing and the women screaming within. There is a large poster of a semi-naked male stripper. We can read the words* **ROMEOS. ONE NIGHT ONLY. WOMEN ONLY.** NATHAN, *Jerry's twelve-year-old son, is looking at it as* **JERRY** *enters*)

JERRY

There you are! You were supposed to wait for me, Nath. I told you it was a short meeting.

(*He re-ties his son's shoelace*)

Did you finish your homework?

NATHAN

(*Of KENO'S picture*)
No, but I know what I want to be when I grow up.

JERRY

Don't be a wiseguy. A good education.

NATHAN

Yes, I finished my homework. You're such a worrier, Dad. Any messages for Mom?

JERRY

Tell her that guy she's living with is still a jerk.

NATHAN

I'm supposed to tell you you're late with this month's payment.

JERRY

I know, I know! I'm working on it. It's not like you're starving.

NATHAN

Don't worry, Dad. You'll get a job.

JERRY

Do I look worried? I'm just waiting for the right situation. You don't want to see your old man bussing tables, do you?

NATHAN

I wouldn't mind.

JERRY

Well he would. You're mine next weekend, remember.

(*Sound of bus*)

There's your bus.

NATHAN

I love you.

(*He kisses JERRY*)

JERRY

Me, too.

(*He lightly punches NATHAN'S arm. This is their ritual*)

Now get outta here before you get me into trouble for keeping you out too late.

NATHAN

Mom's not even home tonight.

(*He goes*)

JERRY

Home! How can he call that place home?

(*He turns to DAVE, who has appeared and stares transfixed at the picture of KENO outside the club*)

Wait'll you have kids, Dave. It changes everything. There's nothing you wouldn't do for your kid. I should've had ten.

DAVE

Why? You're having trouble enough with one. Is that guy for real?

JERRY

We could look like that. It's a choice. Besides, they're all fairies, these Chippendales.

DAVE

They are?

JERRY

Real guys don't look like that. They don't have the time. They look like you.

(Two women hurry on)

SUSAN

Hurry up, it's started!

JOANIE

My sister saw them in Ithaca. She said they were fabulous and she's a lesbian.

JERRY

You really going in there, ladies? What have they got that we don't?

SUSAN

Just about everything. How much do I owe you, Joanie?

JOANIE

Fifty.

(They go into the club)

JERRY

Fifty! Where do these women get that kind of money?

DAVE

Same way we used to. They work for it.

JERRY

Yeah, but fifty bucks! Must be a lot of desperate women in Buffalo.

DAVE

Why not? There's a lot of desperate men.

JERRY

Come on, let's go get drunk.

DAVE

I told Georgie I'd finish the dishes before she got back.

JERRY

Last week I caught you vacuuming. This is not a good trend, Davie.

DAVE

You do housework.

JERRY

That's different. I'm divorced, I have to. Where is Georgie anyway?

DAVE

In there.

JERRY

With those male strippers! You let her go?

DAVE

Jer, she organized it.

JERRY

This is not good at all. All right, this is what you're gonna do! We're gonna walk in that club and you're gonna haul Georgie out of there. Show her who wears the pants in your family.

DAVE

It's women only. How are we gonna get in?

JERRY

Well not through the front door! Follow me.

TRANSITION

(JERRY and DAVE go to the window outside the men's room of the strip club. We hear music and the women cheering off stage. The two men make it through the window with some difficulty)

DAVE

Listen to them in there! It sounds like when the Bills come from behind in the last quarter.

JERRY

I don't know what they're screaming about if they've got the real thing waiting for them at home. You're still giving it to Georgie, aren't you?

DAVE

Of course I am! What do you think I do?

JERRY

I just asked! Best friends get to ask things like that. That's what we're for. Then what the hell is she doing in there?

DAVE

I don't know.

JERRY

You start letting your wife do anything she wants and you're gonna end up like me and Pam.

DAVE

Seems to me like you didn't let Pam do much of anything.

JERRY

Shut up! You don't know squat about me and Pam. Well go on, get her.

DAVE

I'm going, I'm going. You're not coming with me?

JERRY

My wife isn't in there.

DAVE

What if I get caught?

JERRY

No big deal. They'll just castrate you.

(*Sound of raucous* **WOMEN'S** *voices approaching*)

GEORGIE

(*Off*)
That line for the women's room is ridiculous!

DAVE

Jesus Christ! It's my wife!

JERRY

It's the men's room. They wouldn't dare.

(*Door opens*)

GEORGIE

It's empty, what did I tell you?

(*The two men panic and hide in one of the stalls.*

*GEORGIE enters with three friends: ESTELLE
GENOVESE, JOANIE LISH and SUSAN
HERSHEY. They are in high spirits one
moment but can be maudlin the next.
It's the beer.*)

GEORGIE

Ladies, welcome to the inner sanctum of the American male.
Gentlemen, this is a hostile take-over.

SONG: IT'S A WOMAN'S WORLD

GEORGIE
Who's got power?
Who's got juice?
Who's got the money?

JOANIE & ESTELLE
It's a woman's world.

It's a woman's world.
Who feels freedom
To let loose?
Tonight honey-honey

GEORGIE, JOANIE, & ESTELLE
It's a woman's world.

GEORGIE
Back at home my libido is asleep
— Nothing stirring up the batter.
Now I know all I needed was a heap
O' dancing beefcake on a platter.

JOANIE, SUSAN & ESTELLE
A silver platter.

GEORGIE
Let's get sweaty and
Let's get mean.
Fire up the burner —

GEORGIE, JOANIE, SUSAN & ESTELLE
It's a woman's world.

GEORGIE
You be president
You be queen.

JOANIE
I'll be Tina Turner.

WOMEN

It's a woman's world.

GEORGIE

Cause tonight,

SUSAN, JOANIE, & ESTELLE

Yeah tonight,

ALL

It's a woman's world!

JOANIE

This is so cool. Ever since high school I wanted to get a look at the boys' room.

GEORGIE

Why? You just would have seen your phone number all over the wall.

JOANIE

You are such a bitch tonight!

GEORGIE

I know, I love it!

> (*ESTELLE goes to one of the urinals, stands in front of it and pulls down her panty hose. The other women love it!*)

ESTELLE

Look, ma, no hands!

GEORGIE

You didn't learn that one in Girl Scouts.

ESTELLE

I'm standing up for my rights.

THE FULL MONTY

15

GEORGIE

Don't flush! They never do. I say to Davie: "What are you trying
to do? Save water? We got Niagara Falls out there."

GEORGIE

Work all day, I come home, and he's all pissed —
It's a wallow-in-the-mudfest.

Now I know what I need to clear the system's
Just a raunchy little studfest.

God bless their little G-strings!

GEORGIE	**JOANIE, SUSAN, & ESTELLE**
All that music and	*Music*
All that beat,	*Beat*
Who's feeling funny?	*Funny*

ALL

It's a woman's world.

GEORGIE	**JOANIE, SUSAN, & ESTELLE**
All those men moving	*Those men!*
All that meat.	*That meat!*
Tonight, honey honey —	

ALL

It's a woman's world.

SUSAN

I like the chunky little butt
On that motorcycle cop,
I wanna go up there and bite it.

GEORGIE

You'll chip a tooth, honey.

JOANIE

Or G.I. Joe with the military jock,
I'd give a hundred bucks to see what's inside it.

SUSAN &JOANIE

What's inside it.

ESTELLE, SUSAN & JOANIE

What's inside it.
Why do they hide it?

ALL

All that music and
All that beat,
Making me dizzy.
It's a woman's world.

All those men! Moving
All that meat!

GEORGIE

Let's get busy!

ALL

It's a woman's world.
Well it might be the men's room —

GEORGIE

Yeah, but tonight —

ALL

It's a woman's world!
It's a woman's world!
It's a woman's world!
It's a woman's world!

(PAM enters)

PAM

I want somebody to tell me: where were all the men who looked like this when we were in high school? The ass on that UPS driver!

GEORGIE

Pam!

(As they hug)

You can take the girl out of the neighborhood but —

GEORGIE & PAM

You can't take the neighborhood out of the girl!

PAM

When he climbed up on the table and said, "Sign here" I nearly fainted.

SUSAN

Your ex had a beautiful ass, didn't he, Pam?

PAM

Jerry? I don't remember.

ESTELLE

What do you mean "had"? He still does. Oops! Me and my big.

PAM

Hello, Estelle.

ESTELLE

Hello, Mrs. Lukowski. You're the last person in Buffalo I expected to see here tonight.

PAM

Isn't that funny? You're the first.

(ESTELLE, SUSAN & JOANIE exit bathroom)

PAM

I see someone like Estelle and I don't know what Jerry ever saw in me.

GEORGIE

Just about everything. You were so beautiful together. High school sweethearts, that wedding in his mom's backyard, then Nathan. Sometimes I think you and Jerry were the reason me and Davie got married.

PAM

At least you two made it to maturity. We never did. After Nathan was born, one of us had to grow up and it wasn't gonna be Jerry. Nathan needs a father, not a playmate.

(She tries a stall door to find some toilet paper)

Is somebody in there?

JERRY & DAVE

Yes (No), No (Yes).

PAM

Enter Teddy. I never thought I would be living with a man who wore a suit and tie to work. I'm doing yoga. Nathan's started soccer. We're going to Cape Cod next summer. Life's starting to feel real good again, Georgie.

GEORGIE

I hope you're not doing yoga because you're not doing something else.

PAM

I shouldn't have to tell you, Georgie: there's more to a good relationship with a man than sex.

GEORGIE

There is?

PAM

Look at you and Dave.

GEORGIE

All this testosterone in the air has reminded me how long it's been since Davie and I made love.

PAM

Georgie!

GEORGIE

It's making me nuts, Pam. Months and months, not even a hug. I've tried everything from Victoria's Secret to losing fifteen pounds. The girls at work are pushing Prozac on me. I don't need a pill. I need my husband back.

PAM

Georgie, I had no idea.

GEORGIE

My self-esteem would be down to here if it weren't for this guy in shipping who keeps coming on to me.

PAM

But you wouldn't, would you?

GEORGIE

I don't know. He's a black guy. He's married, too. He's pretty good-looking and a great sense of humor. He thinks I'm gorgeous.

PAM

You don't mean that. I know you. You'd never cheat on Dave.

GEORGIE

It's like Davie's given up on everything, including me. I come home to this zombie.

PAM

Dave needs to get back to work. They all do. It was an awful thing, the factory being shut down like that. We're working, they're not — it's not right.

GEORGIE

There's work out there but nothing's good enough for him.

(They go out. There is a long pause. Finally the two men come out of the stall)

JERRY

This was a bad idea.

DAVE

At least you got a nice ass.

JERRY

I'll get a job. I'll show her who Nathan's father is.

DAVE

Georgie says they're going to be hiring at Miracle Mall.

JERRY

Yeah, security guards. Nobody's putting me in a baggy brown uniform so I can walk old ladies to their cars.

DAVE

I hear you.

JERRY

I'll think of something. I'm not going to sit around while my life goes down the drain and my kid gets sold to the highest bidder.

DAVE

That's not what Pam said.

JERRY

It's what she meant! You know how much Cape Cod costs? Come on, let's rob a bank, you fat bastard. I shouldn't call you that. (But you are!)

DAVE

I try to lose weight.

JERRY

What happens?

DAVE

I get hungry and I eat.

JERRY

You eat all you want. You're my kind of guy.

(*They hug as* KENO *enters. He's wearing a leather G-string*)

KENO

Excuse me.

(*He starts to change out of his costume*)

JERRY

Don't get any ideas, prancer.

KENO

I beg your pardon?

JERRY

This is 100% heterosexual prime male you're looking at.

KENO

That's lucky for both of us. You're not my type.

(*Over his shoulder, to Dave*)

Tell your friend he can save the attitude for his number.

DAVE

What number?

KENO

I'm expecting a new dancer. I thought you were his manager, unless it's the other way around. Jesus, that would be a novelty: Benno, the Dancing Belly. No offense.

DAVE

My name's not Benno and he's not a stripper.

KENO

Then what the hell are you two doing in here? It's Ladies Only.

JERRY

What are you, pretty boy?

KENO

I'm what the ladies wish you looked like.

JERRY

We're what the ladies don't know you're not.

KENO

I know what you're going to say.

JERRY & KENO

Real men.

KENO

Get a life.

JERRY

Don't worry, I will!

KENO

What's his problem anyway?

JERRY
You are, flyboy!

(*He takes a swing at* **KENO,** *who easily catches his arm and sends* **JERRY** *flying*)

KENO
Fairies: One; Bigots: Zero.

DAVE
Jesus, Jerry! What did he do?

JERRY
He took me for one of them.

DAVE
He took me for your manager. I'm the one who ought to take a swing at him.

KENO
(*Ready for* **DAVE,** *too*)
Come on, doughboy. You want to mix it up?

DAVE
This is getting silly. I'm sorry. We're both in a very emotional state. We just found out what our wives really thought of us. Well, my wife; his ex.

KENO
I think you're both pathetic.

DAVE
That's sort of what they said. We've been unemployed almost eighteen months. It gets to you after a while.

KENO
That's why my brother split to Albany. He couldn't take it here anymore.

(DAVE is trying to clean JERRY'S cut lip with a wet paper towel)

JERRY

Ow!

DAVE

Well stand still!

KENO

Is he gonna live?

JERRY

I'm fine. You're just lucky I didn't see you coming.

KENO

I know, I'm a very lucky girl. I gotta show to do. This time I'm John Wayne. Go figure. Listen, it beats working at a mall.

DAVE

That's what Jerry always says, except we're not working.

JERRY

What's your brother doing in Albany?

KENO

Working at a mall, honey.

(He goes)

DAVE

He seemed like a decent guy.

JERRY

He called me honey. Did you hear that? Creeped me out.

DAVE

I thought it was kind of nice.

You! You cry at *Wheel of Fortune*! Come on, let's get out of here.

(*DAVE makes a thrusting movement with his pelvis*)

What the hell are you doing?

DAVE

You heard him: He thought we were some of them Chippendales.

JERRY

Do that again.

DAVE

Why? Am I turning you on, darling?

(*DAVE makes another pelvic thrust*)

JERRY

Yes!

DAVE

I didn't know you cared, Jerry.

JERRY

You're giving me one hell of an idea. If our ladies are spending fifty bucks a pop to see total strangers dancing around in the raw, can you imagine what they'd spend to see the likes of you and me?

DAVE

Yeah, nothing!

JERRY

They'd melt at the sight of us, a couple of home boys baring their all. And we're straight, too!

(*Cheers and yells from the women inside the club*)

JERRY

That could be us they're screaming for. Real men this time. Not somebody on a poster all perfect but a guy you could see walking the streets of Buffalo.

DAVE

Yeah, out of work, picking his nose, scratching his ass.

(*MUSIC begins*)

JERRY

You have no imagination.

DAVE

And you are out of your mind! Guys like us, stripping!

SONG: MAN

JERRY

You're out of work. Your pride is missin'.
They call you jerk, but you don't listen.
You haven't got a pot to piss in
But you're a...man.

(*As JERRY fantasizes their new career identities,*
we make a transition to outside the back of
Tony Giordano's club)

· *Your hands are rough. Your back is hairy.*
Your talk is tough. Your smell is scary.
Here's what you're not — you're not a fairy.
No, you're a beer-drinking, real live man.

And when the beef comes out, you do the carvin'.
You hate Tom Cruise but you love Lee Marvin.

You're a man. And that's a bonus
'Cause when you're swinging your cojones
You'll show 'em what testosterone is —
'Cause you're a boot-wearin', beer-drinking, Chevy-driving man.

Don't do it to be the most talked-about man in Buffalo. Don't do it for all the money you're gonna rake in. Don't even do it so your best friend can keep seeing his son, whom he loves more than life. Oh no! Do it for yourself, Davie-boy. Show yourself the stuff you're made of. Don't show me.

DAVE

You're wasting your breath.

JERRY

It's a brilliant plan. My best one ever.

DAVE

You get these plans. They always fail.
You've been divorced. You've been to jail.
You may be bold. You may be male,
But you're a… bum bum ba-dum BUM!
You got your dreams, you got your wishes,
And I don't want to sound malicious
But you're a nut, and I got dishes —
I'm going home.

JERRY

You walk away now but you'll be back. You know you're always there for me.

DAVE

Not this time, Fabio. Jerry the stripper!

(*He goes.* JERRY *continues his reverie*)

JERRY

Surf's up, ladies! Here comes Lukowski — the Big Kahuna — riding your pipeline! I'm hanging ten.

Stand back, ladies. Quarterback Jerry, throwing a long one right into your end zone! Touchdown!

Bases loaded, it's Bad Boy Jerry, swinging a big, big bat. Banging one right at you, baby! Boo Yaa!

I'm gonna jump straight up, kick a hole in the moon.
Don't know exactly where I'm going
But I know I'm gonna get there soon.
I'll show you. I'll show them all.
I'll show them all the real thing.

What is a man? Why does he bother?
'Cause he's a man. 'Cause he's a father.
He wants his kid. He wants his life. He wants to be a man —
A real man. Yes I am.
I wanna be. I gotta be —

A real man with a mission
Like you see on television,
I'm a real fine gen-u-ine —
Man!

> (**KENO** *is coming out of the club surrounded by adoring*
> **WOMEN**. *He is dressed in street clothes. He carries his*
> *costumes in a garment bag. He signs autographs.*
> *He poses for pictures.* **JERRY** *observes and glowers*)

KENO
Thank you, ladies. You're too much.

JOANIE
Get our picture, Dolores!

SUSAN
(*Holding a bright yellow G-string*)
I'm gonna ask my husband to put this on. I haven't had a good laugh since our last anniversary.

SECOND STRIPPER

Keno, I'll get the van!

(The other women surge toward him as he leaves)

JOANIE

Look, there's the Roman gladiator.

SUSAN

Hey, wait for us.

*(The WOMEN move off after the other DANCER.
KENO is used to being dropped like this.
Suddenly he and JERRY are alone)*

KENO

(To JERRY)
It's not easy being someone's fantasy. People forget you have feelings and you end up feeling like a piece of meat.

JERRY

Do you think I'm attractive?

KENO

Somehow I didn't expect you to ask me that. Sorry, I've got a boyfriend.

JERRY

No, I mean do you think they'd think I was sexy?

KENO

Who? The ladies? You don't know?

JERRY

I mean if I did what you did? If I, you know...

(He makes a pelvic thrust)

KENO

I think people would think you were pretty funny. Or scary even. But not sexy.

JERRY

How do you get to be sexy?

KENO

The same way you get to Carnegie Hall: practice, lots of practice.

JERRY

You don't think I got what it takes?

KENO

Anybody can take their clothes off. But to do it on a stage, with hundreds and hundreds of people looking at you, yeah, that takes something.

JERRY

What? Tell me.

KENO

I'll let you find out.

(*He hears the van horn*)

Utica, here I come! Everybody wants to be in show business.

(*He goes, leaving* JERRY *more frustrated than ever*)

I'm gonna jump straight up, kick a hole in the moon.
Don't know exactly where I'm going but I know
I'm gonna get there!
I may be broke. I may be lazy.
Might be a joke or fucking crazy.
But I'm a man. Yeah, I'm a man...

TRANSITION

*(Day. Two **MEN** are on the street.*
This is what we hear of their conversation)

MARTY

Woke up to another "for sale" sign this morning. This one was right next door.

REG

The Carlucci's? Dan and Louise? They're third generation Buffalo.

MARTY

Moving to Raleigh, as soon as they sell.

REG

They should make a bumper sticker. Buffalo: Love it and leave it.

MARTY

What happened? This used to be a great town.

REG

It will be again. You know the saying: The grass is always greener.

MARTY

What grass? We got contaminated brownfield.

*(They are gone. **JERRY** storms up to*
***TEDDY SLAUGHTER** and **PAM'S** front*
door and bangs on it. He has a sheaf of legal-
*looking papers. **PAM** opens the door)*

JERRY

(At once)
So what's all this about a deadline and you having sole custody? That wasn't the deal, Pam.

PAM

If you want joint custody, Jerry, you're going to have to pay your share. Seven hundred dollars a month. That was the deal. You've been in arrears since it started.

JERRY

I'm on the unemployment line in case you haven't heard!

PAM

Then get a job. I'll *give* you a job.

JERRY

Nine-fifty an hour in the Black Hole of fucking Calcutta. No thank you.

PAM

It's not the Black Hole of Calcutta and I'll thank you to stop using that kind of language when you're here.

JERRY

Niagara Estates, I'm very impressed!

PAM

Nathan comes home from you talking like a sailor.

JERRY

Pam, have you ever met a sailor?

PAM

Teddy doesn't appreciate it either.

JERRY

That wuss! Where is he?

PAM

Right inside.

JERRY

Working on his stamp collection?

PAM

Fine. Whatever. If you want to go off and play your games, you do that, Jerry. But from now on Nathan's going to have two parents.

JERRY

That would be your stud lover. And abracadabra and here he is. Hello, Teddy.

(*TEDDY has appeared at the doorway, next to PAM*)

PAM

The court will decide who Nath's parents are.

JERRY

No, it won't. Nathan's yours and he's mine and he's fuck all to do with him.

TEDDY

As if you've ever given a damn.

PAM

Jerry, Nathan doesn't even like staying at your place. He says it's a mess and he's cold all the time.

JERRY

We have fun. Where is he? Up in his room?

(*He yells up to the bedroom windows*)

Hey, Nath! We have a good time together, don't we, son?

PAM

Jerry, don't.

JERRY

Is he home? Don't we, Nath? Tell 'em. Please.

(*No one comes to the window*)

He can't hear me through all your double-glazed windows, Teddy.

PAM
(*Gently*)
He can hear.

TEDDY
Actually they're triple-glazed, Jerry.

PAM
Don't, Teddy. I want you to have your time with Nath, Jerry, but I want you to keep our agreement, too.

(*She goes into the house*)

JERRY
This is fucked. I'm his dad and you — you're nobody.

TEDDY
I've asked Pam to marry me. If she says yes, this business of child support becomes rather academic, doesn't it? So long, Jerry.

(*He shuts the door on him*)

JERRY
Nobody!

(*Looks up at the window again. Then, with forced cheerfulness*)

So long, son. See you soon.

TRANSITION

(*A city park. A couple powerwalks by as NATHAN jogs into view. He has his school things in his knapsack*)

NATHAN

Come on, Dad, catch up! I don't have all morning.

(*An exhausted JERRY jogs into view*)

JERRY

Why do we have to run so fast?

NATHAN

It's called exercise.

JERRY

(*Winded*)
Dave's the one you should be yelling at. We left him back at the 7-11.

NATHAN

Are you really going to do this stripping thing?

JERRY

You got a better idea? I only have two weeks to get the money or I lose you.

NATHAN

Couldn't you just get a normal job?

JERRY

They take too long. I need a one-night killing.

NATHAN

Dad, just promise you won't tell anybody what you're gonna do. I mean, anybody I know. Okay?

JERRY

You gonna be ashamed of me?

NATHAN

I could never be ashamed of you.

JERRY
That's my boy.

NATHAN
It's more like embarrassed. I'm gonna be late. See you.

(*He jogs off as* **DAVE** *huffs and puffs into view*)

JERRY
That a boy, Dave. Our first day and you look better already.

DAVE
Save the sweet talk. I'm not doing it, Jerry. I'll train with you but I'm not taking my clothes off in front of a thousand women. Hell, I don't even like to take my clothes off in front of Georgie.

JERRY
We can make a lot of money. Fifty thousand easy.

DAVE
You can make a lot of money. I'm keeping my pants on. Just call me Tina Turner: I'm a private dancer. Give me a cigarette.

JERRY
We're in training.

DAVE
You promised me a cigarette if I made it up this hill.

JERRY
I meant the next hill.

DAVE
Bastard.

(*They jog off as the speed walkers return. They are thoroughly winded now. All their enthusiasm is gone. This time they speed trudge*)

TRANSITION

(We see a small parked car with its engine running as JERRY and DAVE jog into view)

JERRY

Think of all those women lusting for your luscious body!

DAVE

The only thing I'm lusting for is a smoke!

(DAVE peels away from JERRY, who keeps running)

JERRY

Come on, Dave, we only got another mile.

DAVE

Bastard!

(DAVE knocks on the driver's side window. He is utterly oblivious to the hose-pipe that goes from the exhaust into the car via the passenger window, not to mention the fumes building up inside.

At the wheel is MALCOLM)

DAVE

You got a cigarette? That bastard won't give me one.

(MALCOLM hands him a whole pack through the sunroof)

DAVE

Thanks.

(MALCOLM closes the roof)

You got a light?

(MALCOLM gives him a lighter)

Much obliged.

TERRENCE MCNALLY & DAVID YAZBEK

JERRY
(*Calling from a little distance*)
Come on, Dave, we're almost there!

(*He stops to catch his breath*)

DAVE
(*Leaning towards* MALCOLM)
Hey, weren't you at the factory before it closed?

(MALCOLM *nods dumbly*)

I thought I recognized you. You were on the floor with Jerry.
That's him up the road. How's it going?

(MALCOLM *slumps forward*)

Nice talking to you, too.

(*He shakes his head and jogs up to* JERRY)

JERRY
The Good Samaritan, leave it to you.

DAVE
I don't know what he's so bummed out about. He's the only guy
who got a job out of the plant closing. They made him the night
security guard.

(*A sudden and violent realization*)

Holy shit!

(*He runs to the car,* JERRY *hard on his heels. They pull*
MALCOLM, *coughing and sputtering, out and lay him on*
the ground. DAVE *desperately gasps for air after so much*
exertion, bellowing in pain and exhaustion)

DAVE

It's MacGregor. MacGregor, open your eyes. Are you all right?

MALCOLM

Leave me alone, you bastard.

DAVE

Who are you calling a bastard? I just saved your life! Okay, you asked for it.

(DAVE picks MALCOLM up by the trousers, hurls him back into the car and slams the door. He leans against the door, drinking in the air, while pointedly ignoring the frantic knocking on the window)

JERRY

What are you trying to do? Kill him?

DAVE

I'm tired of everyone calling me a bastard.

JERRY

Then stop acting like one. Let him out of there.

(They pull MALCOLM out of the car. JERRY turns off the ignition. They collapse by the side of the road. They are all exhausted. They huff and puff and stare up at the sky)

MALCOLM

Thanks.

JERRY

Don't mention it. We do that for everyone we see trying to commit suicide.

DAVE

Cigarette?

TERRENCE MCNALLY & DAVID YAZBEK

MALCOLM

No thanks, I'm trying to quit.

JERRY

If you're serious about killing yourself —

MALCOLM

I am!

JERRY

— then you wanna find a nice high bridge, like one of them bungee jumps, only without the bungee bit.

MALCOLM

I'm afraid of heights.

DAVE

Drowning! Now there's a great way to go! Very peaceful, I heard. Fill your pockets with rocks, wade on out into Lake Erie.

MALCOLM

I can't swim.

JERRY

You don't have to swim to drown, you jerk. You're not too bright, are you?

MALCOLM

My mother would agree with you.

JERRY

And you listen to her?

MALCOLM

I live with her.

JERRY

That would drive me to suicide.

MALCOLM

She's not well. She needs me.

JERRY

So who's going to take care of her when you're gone?

MALCOLM

I hadn't thought about that.

DAVE

I know! Go stand in the middle of the Thruway and get a friend to run you over really fast.

JERRY

Good thinking, Dave. That should do it.

MALCOLM

I don't have any friends.

(*JERRY rolls on top of* MALCOLM *and pulls his head up by the hair*)

JERRY

Listen, you, we just saved your life, so don't tell us you don't have any friends!

DAVE

(*Over him, too*)
Me, too! I'd as soon run you over as look at you.

MALCOLM

I'm sorry.

JERRY

What are friends for? Who else is gonna help you kill yourself?

SONG: BIG-ASS ROCK

Let's find a rock —
I mean a big-ass rock.
Or maybe something like a cinderblock is better.
I'll hoist it up
And drop it on your face, my buddy.

And just before the lights go out
You'll see my smile and you'll know you've got a friend
With a rock
Who cares.
I mean a big-ass rock.

DAVE

Or rope.
I got some quality rope
Made for a man who's devoid of hope like you are,
My buddy…
Michael —

MALCOLM

Unh, that's Malcolm.

DAVE

Malcolm. Right, right.

And I won't leave you swinging there,
Twitching like a fish while you claw the air.
I'll grab your feet
And pal o' mine,
I'll pull real hard
And SNAP your spinal cord.

JERRY

This world is cold when you're alone and they ignore you
But don't kill yourself.

JERRY & DAVE

We'll do it for you.
You've got a friend.

JERRY
You've got a friend.

DAVE
You've got a friend.

DAVE
I asked a guy once if he'd mind putting me in a barrel and sending me over the falls. You know what the son of a bitch said? "Fuck you, asshole."

JERRY
People are pricks. I asked a guy to take his air-compressor and drill me with a six-inch nail right through the eye.

DAVE
What'd he say?

JERRY
"I'm low on nails."

DAVE
People are selfish pricks.

JERRY
Another time, now get this, I lay down in front of a steam roller and asked this guy just to proceed, you know, business as usual, and just squash me like a bug.

DAVE
That's a good way to go, Jer, the ol' bug squash.

MALCOLM
You mean you guys think about killing yourselves, too?

JERRY
About once a day.

MALCOLM

What stops you?

JERRY

He tells me it would break his heart.

DAVE

(*Coolly looking at* MALCOLM)
We could tie a plastic laundry bag over his head.

JERRY

Naw, that's such a wimp suicide.

MALCOLM

I put my finger in a socket once. It hurt real bad but it didn't kill me.

JERRY

Malcolm, stay out of this.

MALCOLM	DAVE & JERRY
I've got a friend,	*Ooh…*
Like Carol King	
(Or was it Carly Simon) used to sing?	
I always get those two confused.	
But anyway—	
	DAVE & JERRY
I turned around and suddenly	*Aah…*
I'm not alone, it ain't just me.	*Ooh…*
I'm like a player on the team —	
	Player on our team.
I'm part of the gang…	
	Part of the gang.
MALCOLM	**JERRY & DAVE**
A member of the club.	
	Welcome to the club.

DAVE

Ooh…let's get a club.

JERRY

I like the big-ass rock.

DAVE

Naw, one good swing and I'll clean his clock forever.

JERRY

Let gravity do the work.

DAVE

It's a man's way to die, Mikey.

JERRY

Malcolm!

JERRY & DAVE	MALCOLM
	I got friends!
Friends who will love you	
Like a maniac —	
And lead you like a lamb to	
The railroad track	*Ooh…*
And tie you down.	
	I got friends!
Or tickle your wrist with a single-edge razor	
Or buy you a beer with a draino chaser	
Or dump you in the river with a rock…	

MALCOLM

A *big-ass* rock!

(JERRY is trying to pick up a big rock)

JERRY

Here's a nice one right over here.

DAVE

Can I give you a hand with that? It looks heavy.

JERRY

No Dave,

It ain't heavy…he's my friend.

DAVE

Come on, group hug!

(*They both hug* **MALCOLM**)

JERRY

I've been thinking, Malcolm: A body like yours must drive the ladies crazy.

DAVE

Oh God…here we go again.

MALCOLM

Really? My mother says I'm pigeon-chested.

JERRY

And I bet you move like a bat out of hell, too.

MALCOLM

I've only danced with my mom. When she's well, she likes to dance.

JERRY

You know what a pelvic thrust is, Malcolm?

DAVE

Don't listen to him, buddy! He'll have you buck naked in no time.

JERRY

It's as easy as falling off a log.

(**MALCOLM** *imitates the movement*)

THE FULL MONTY

47

Yeah, okay. You're hired.

> (**MALCOLM**, *aglow with the realization that he has found*
> *two men who might actually become real friends,*
> *works on his pelvic thrust. A lifetime of loneliness*
> *is being released. He is on another "plane" from*
> **JERRY** *and* **DAVE**. *He doesn't hear the following*)

DAVE	MALCOLM
	I've got friends...
What do you want him for?	
His mother is right.	
He *is* pigeon-chested	*Ooh...*
and he's suicidal.	

JERRY

He's the night security guard at the plant. We'll have a place to practice.

DAVE

Quit saying "we," will you?

JERRY	MALCOLM
Besides, it'll be good	
what-do-you-call-it for him?	
Therapy!	*Ooh...I've got — !*

DAVE	MALCOLM
Oh, sure.	*I've got friends...*

JERRY

Much better, Malcolm! You're a natural. Now don't ask too many questions. Remember, tomorrow night, eight o'clock sharp, practice at the plant.

MALCOLM

I'm not supposed to let anyone in there.

TERRENCE MCNALLY & DAVID YAZBEK

JERRY

Malcolm, we're friends. Friends don't say no to friends.

DAVE

McGregor, you're gonna wish I'd *left* you in that car.

(*He moves away, shaking his head*)

JERRY

Eight o'clock. Don't be late.

MALCOLM

I can't be late. I'm the night guard.

(*JERRY high-fives him. MALCOLM is ecstatic. He fairly skips home*)

I've got friends...

Ooh...I've got —

TRANSITION

(*His buoyant spirits are instantly deflated by what awaits him: his old mother, MOLLY, who sits confined to a wheelchair she is painfully struggling to get out of*)

MALCOLM

What are you doing?

MOLLY

(*Waving him away*)
I can manage. I don't need you to get up to my own bed.

MALCOLM

I'm sorry. I lost track of time.

MOLLY
What were you doing?

MALCOLM
Just hanging out, with some friends.

MOLLY
You don't have any friends, Malcolm.

MALCOLM
I do now.

MOLLY
Well don't let me get in the way.

MALCOLM
It won't happen again.

(*Silence. Each understands the other*)

MOLLY
I thought you'd gone.

(**MALCOLM** *shakes his head*)

MOLLY
You going to leave me here all day?

(*He picks her up and carries her in his arms*)

MALCOLM

It's okay now.

MOLLY
I hope they're nice boys, Malcolm.

TRANSITION

(*At once, ballroom music is heard. **HAROLD NICHOLS** and his wife, **VICKI NICHOLS**, dance into view. **JERRY**, **DAVE**, **MALCOLM**, and **NATHAN** enter and watch from the sidelines*)

DANCE INSTRUCTOR
Cha cha time, Mr. and Mrs. Nichols. Feel that Latin beat!

JERRY
If that's dancing, I'd rather not. They'd laugh us off the stage if we pulled that. Can't you just see us, Dave?

NATHAN
It's a dance school and you said you were looking for a teacher.

JERRY
Thanks, Nath, but it's just not the sort of dancing we need. This is more for a cruise ship. Let's go.

DAVE
Jer, wait, look at those two! They're terrific.

JERRY
(*Watching **HAROLD** and **VICKI** a beat*)
Distinct possibilities.

(***HAROLD** has **VICKI** in an impressive dip.*

*When he lets her up, he comes face to face With **JERRY** and the others.*

*It is hard to say who is more startled at the mutual recognition: **HAROLD** or **JERRY**. Nonetheless, **HAROLD** nearly drops **VICKI** at the sight of his former nemesis*)

JERRY

Oh no, Harold the Hun!

VICKI

Harold, what's the matter? You look like you've seen a ghost.

MALCOLM

Hi, Mr. Nichols, remember us?

JERRY

What are you doing?

MALCOLM

That's Mr. Nichols, we know him.

JERRY

Of course we know him. That's the SOB who cost-efficienced us right out of our jobs.

VICKI

Who are they, Harold?

DAVE

He lost his, too.

JERRY

Serves him right, the bastard. Let's get out of here!!

HAROLD

Just some rollers from the plant. One of them is a real trouble-maker. Come on, let's dance.

VICKI

Wait! Maybe something's wrong, Harold.

HAROLD

Vicki!
(But she is already going over to the men)

TERRENCE McNALLY & DAVID YAZBEK

VICKI

Hello, I'm Vicki Nichols, Mr. Nichols' wife. Is everything all right at the plant?

JERRY

What plant?

HAROLD

I'm sure things at the plant are fine, Vicki.

(*Between clenched teeth*)

She doesn't know. She doesn't know.

JERRY

What do you mean she doesn't know?

HAROLD

That I was let go, too. You gotta cover for me, please.

JERRY

It's not about the plant, Mrs. Nichols. This is more of a social visit.

VICKI

That's a relief. You caught us brushing up our Latin dancing before Harold takes me to Puerto Rico next month. Have you been? Daiquiris to die for. Of course, Bali is our dream destination. See Bali and die, n'est-ce pas?

DAVE

That's what I always say.

VICKI

With jobs like yours you have to travel. Harold comes home beat, the weight of the world on his shoulders, and all he thinks of is where to take me next. You know him as Mr. Nichols, supervisor. I know him as Harold, the perfect husband.

HAROLD

Vicki!

VICKI

I love to make him blush. Then don't listen, Harold.

SONG: LIFE WITH HAROLD

You gotta love that man,
He's like my personal angel.
I've always wanted the kind of life
That I've been having as Harold's wife.
What a catch I have caught.
He would buy me the moon if the moon could be bought.
I'm telling you —
You gotta love that man.

JERRY

Why can't you just tell her?

HAROLD

She adores me. How do you break the heart of someone you love?

VICKI

I really love that man.
He likes me dressed to the nines.
I say two words and then "ta-da"
There's me completely in Prada.
And I've got the boots that go with the belt
That goes with the bag
That goes with my wonderful life with Harold.
You gotta love that man.

Harold told me you boys are rollers at the mill. That's wonderful.
Of course I still don't know what rollers do. I hardly know what
Harold does. It's all steel to me.

HAROLD
Look at her. She's a piece of Dresden China. She'd break into a
million pieces.

VICKI
God, I love that man.
But lately he's working too hard.
I keep telling him how we
Deserve a few weeks in Maui.
And we'll feel the breeze and sample the poi
And go see Don Ho and I'll say
"Oh boy, how I love you, Harold."
I hit the jackpot with Harry.

He's a gem. He's a beaut.
He looks cute in a suit and he loves me to boot.

I'm telling you —	### DAVE & MALCOLM
You gotta love that man,	*Love that man.*
Love that man	*You gotta love that man.*
I love that man.	*You really gotta love*
I love that man.	*That man.*

JERRY
Malcolm, dance with Mrs. Nichols while we have a word with
Mr. Nichols.

MALCOLM
I only know how to follow, Mrs. Nichols.

VICKI
(Always ready for a good time)
That's all right, Malcolm, I only know how to lead.

(MALCOLM and VICKI will continue to dance back and forth
during the following)

HAROLD
What is this all about? I know you don't like me but I hope you'll
consider my wife's feelings.

JERRY

We need your help, Mr. Nichols.

HAROLD

I'm sorry but at this point in my life I'm trying to help myself. It's sink or swim time and I'm drowning. It's every man for himself.

JERRY

We want to learn to dance. We need a teacher.

HAROLD

Dance? Wouldn't you be better off looking for a job like I am?

JERRY

This is a job, sort of. We're gonna strip. We want you teach us.

HAROLD

Strip? Like a Chippendale's thing?

JERRY

More like a Buffalo version. More realistic, more...masculine! Over at Tony Giordano's place, we figure we can make 50 thou. One night only.

HAROLD

But you can't dance.

JERRY

That's where you come in.

HAROLD

Now I've heard everything!

JERRY

What's so funny?

HAROLD

I can just see you, the Three Stooges, prancing around Buffalo with your willies out. What are you gonna call yourselves? The dancing dicks? Peanut size, I'm sure. Bring your own telescope.

JERRY

I knew you wouldn't help us. We'll do it without you.

HAROLD

No, you won't. You won't do it at all!

JERRY

Why not, Mr. Nichols? Just why the hell not?

HAROLD

I'll tell you, Lukowski. 'Cause you're too thin, he's too fat, he's too dumb and you're all too ugly.

JERRY

(Calling to VICKI)
Mrs. Nichols — !

HAROLD

No! It'll kill her. Who am I kidding? It'll kill me.

(He starts to break down)

JERRY

(Unprepared for this)
Hey!

HAROLD

You don't know what it's like, what I'm going through. I was somebody before this happened.

JERRY

(Gently)
We know, Mr. Nichols. So were we.

HAROLD

I have an MBA from the Wharton School of Business. I can't take the first thing that comes along. But you! You're kids. You think it's all a game. I can't run out and steal a car like you, Lukowski, and go to jail. I've got a standard of living. Responsibilities.

DAVE

So do we. Tell him about Nath.

(*To* HAROLD)

Mr. Nichols, Jerry'll lose joint custody of his son if he doesn't come up with his share of money. You don't have kids. The way you love your missus is how Jerry loves Nath, maybe only even more.

JERRY

Why'd you have to go telling him that? He doesn't care.

HAROLD

Fifty thousand, you said?

JERRY
(*Seizing the opportunity*)
Fifty thou, easy.

HAROLD
(*Wavering*)
It's not my kind of dancing. It's just ass-wiggling. Anybody can...

(*He gives his version of a pelvic thrust*)

JERRY
(*Pouncing*)
If it was just ass-wiggling we wouldn't need your help.

HAROLD

What if someone finds out? I've got a reputation to protect.

JERRY
You've also got a stack of bills and a wife who likes to go places, Harold.

HAROLD
Harold?

JERRY
(Blithely)
That's all right, you can call me Jerry.

HAROLD
I'm a son of a bitch to take orders from.

JERRY
We know that. You should have heard some of the names we had for you.

DAVE
Horrible Harold. Harold Hitler.

JERRY
Not now, Dave. Now how many other guys you figure we need to put on a good show?

HAROLD
Minimum six, unless you want us looking at your skinny legs all night.

> *(Other MEN are dancing by with their partners. HAROLD is already sizing them up for their potential as performers)*

HAROLD
There's a possibility. Ask him if wants to strip.

JERRY
You ask him.

HAROLD

That's what producers do, isn't it? Ask people to take their clothes off.

JERRY

Not men!

HAROLD

It's very simple. You go up to him and say, "Excuse me, you're a good-looking man. My friends and I are putting on a show and wonder how you'd feel about dropping your trousers for us?" There's nothing to it.

(They all watch the man dancing. A YOUNG WOMAN comes up to JERRY, who for once does not perk up at the sight and sound of an attractive woman)

YOUNG WOMAN

You wanna dance?

JERRY

Not now, sweetheart. I'm busy.

(To the others)

Do we like the ass on that guy?

HAROLD

I've seen better. You can't rush this.

(Another YOUNG MAN dances by with his partner)

DAVE

Jer, look, a possible nine.

JERRY

Hell, Dave, that guy's a ten!

(He turns. YOUNG WOMAN does a take and leaves)

TRANSITION

(As the dancers swirl away, NATHAN is seen handing out flyers. We also see a hand-lettered poster. We can make out one word in big letters: AUDITIONS)

WOMAN

Look, Betty. Tryouts for male strippers.

BETTY

At least it's not another production of *The Velveteen Rabbit.*

WOMAN

Buffalo. We gave the world Buffalo wings. Now we're gonna give 'em Buffalo wieners. This I gotta see.

(Two MEN are reading NATHAN'S flyers)

MAN

"Male Strippers. Tryouts tonight. No experience necessary." They gotta be kidding.

OTHER MAN

I'd pay a good fifty to see you wiggling your wick, Jackson.

(To NATHAN)

Does your father know what you're doing, kid?

NATHAN

Yeah! He organized it. You coming to tryouts?

MAN

Get outta here!

OTHER MAN

What is Buffalo coming to?

MAN

Desperate times take desperate measures.

TRANSITION

(*We are in the abandoned factory's security
area, MALCOLM'S domain. Auditions
are in progress.*

*JERRY, DAVE, MALCOLM, HAROLD
and NATHAN are sitting behind a long table.
Waiting patiently at a battered upright piano,
wreathed in smoke from the cigarette that is
always in her mouth, is JEANETTE BURMEISTER.*

*A man has just finished. From their expressions,
he has made little impression*)

JERRY
(*Referring to an index card*)
Thank you, Mr....

MAN
You can call me Marty.

JERRY
Thank you, Marty.

MAN
I also do this thing with a bullwhip. You know, crack it.

HAROLD
Thank you. We'll be in touch.

MAN
I guess that's a "no?" Thank you.

(*MAN trudges off. It's a tragic, hopeless exit*)

JERRY
I feel terrible. He's got four kids. Couldn't he — ?

HAROLD

No! There's got to be a modicum of talent, Jerry.

DAVE

Why don't we ask the piano player?

JERRY

What did you think, Jeanette?

JEANETTE

You talking to me?

JERRY

What did you think of him?

JEANETTE

No sense of rhythm, sings flat and a bad toupee. Other than that, I'd grab him.

JERRY

We're running out of possibilities.

JEANETTE

Don't worry. When the right guy walks through that door, you'll know it. He'll glimmer. He'll light up the room. I've seen it happen a thousand times. You audition for days, they're all dogs, you're ready to slit your wrists, and in walks Barbra Streisand!

HAROLD

Who is this person?

JERRY

She just showed up, piano and all.

JEANETTE

Besides, you're offering these guys more than a job. You're offering them hope. I'll tell you this: *my* heart beat a little faster when I heard about this gig. I said to my husband, Lou, Lou Feltzer, (he had a minor hit with "Milkman's Serenade" on Decca in 1947 — if you listen close you can hear me tickling the ivories on the third chorus), I said, "Lou, wake up! I'm tired of sitting and rocking, aren't you? We may be retired and living in Buffalo (which is probably an oxymoron) but I haven't milked my last cow yet. Some boys from the old mill are putting on a show. Send me my mail there."

(*The MEN just look at her*)

All right, who's next? I'm ready to rock and roll!

(*Another MAN enters. It's REG WILLOUGHBY*)

REG
Hi, guys, remember me?

(*General greetings*)

I thought I'd give it a go. It said amateur. You can't be any more amateur than this. Hit it!

JEANETTE
Hit what, sweetheart?

REG
Do you know any "Heartbreak Hotel?"

JEANETTE
Honey, I wrote it! Do me a favor, try to keep up.

> (*She bangs out a "strip" version of one of Elvis' biggest hits. REG begins to strip. He undresses about as unerotically as most men undress for bed. The Gang watches, open-mouthed. Even JEANETTE stops playing in disbelief. REG gets his trousers halfway down before coming to a halt. Sadly, he shakes his head and pulls them up again*)

REG

Sorry, I...sorry. Thought I'd give it a try. Things being a bit desperate. I don't have to tell you how it is. Three boys to feed and I can't even take my clothes off properly.

(*He's on the edge*)

JERRY

It's okay, Reg, no problem. You want a beer?

REG

No, thanks, Jerry. I got the kids outside.

JERRY

Bring 'em in.

REG

This is no place for kids. Thanks.

HAROLD

Thank you, Mr. Willoughby.

(*He goes. Long, depressed silence*)

JEANETTE

Why do the really bad ones always have kids? If you want to be in show business, you should be spayed first.

JERRY

Couldn't —

HAROLD

No! You heard the lady. She said a *glimmer*, Jerry!

(*HORSE enters. He seems very old and frail for the assignment*)

HORSE

Hello.

HAROLD

He's too old.

JERRY
(*Ignoring this, looking at HORSE's card*)
Your name is Mr. Horse.

HORSE

No, just Horse.

JERRY

You want to tell us something about yourself, Horse?

HORSE

What do you want to know? I'm out of work. They let me go at McDonald's. Said I wasn't cheerful enough. Scaring the customers. Since my wife passed, I've been living with my aunt. She's got leukemia. Stuff like that?

JERRY

That will be fine. Horse, just let my colleagues on the panel and I...Jeanette!

JEANETTE

This is the part where they talk about you and you have to pretend you don't hear. I remember you at McDonald's. I was waitressing at the IHOP across the street.

(*HORSE talks to JEANETTE while others confer in whispers*)

JERRY

Now this is more like it.

DAVE

An old man?

JERRY

No, dolt, a *black* man. They're every woman's fantasy. Ask him *why* he's called Horse.

DAVE

You ask him. It's not 'cause he runs the Kentucky Derby.

HAROLD

What's the use of a big bundle if you need a walker to carry it around. He must be fifty if he's a day.

JERRY

So, Horse, what, uh, can you do?

HORSE

Well there's the Bump, the Stomp, the Twist. My break-dancing days are probably over but there's always the Funky Chicken.

JERRY

There you go, Horse. One Funky Chicken, Jeanette.

JEANETTE

To stay or to go?

HORSE

It's been a while, remember. And I've got this dicey hip.

JEANETTE

Tally ho, Horse. Let's blow their minds.

> (*JEANETTE begins to play. Almost at once, the orchestra will cut in. This will always be true when JEANETTE plays.*
>
> *HORSE begins to dance, painfully, slowly at first. The Gang can barely conceal their disappointment and irritation. Another waste of time!*

*But then **HORSE** lets the music flow through*
his bones, old limbs are remembering old
sequences, and before you know it, he is
grooving, spinning, twisting and funking that
chicken like there is no tomorrow)

SONG: BIG BLACK MAN

HORSE
When I was just a little nipper daddy told me "Son,
That thing there underneath your zipper can be lots of fun.
When you get a little older, you'll understand
That every woman in the world loves a big black man."

Now I ain't elite, I ain't no man of means
But I got mean feet and my daddy's genes.
You just meet me once and you'll understand
There ain't nothing in the world like a big black man.

'Cause I'm big and I'm proud,
Singing out loud.
Dancing it since the day I was born.

Who's got the tools?
Who breaks the rules?
'Git back
And let a man do the Popcorn.

I'm what your sister and your mother's always thinking of,
They put my picture on the cover of the book of love.
Never need a line,
I don't need no plan,
'Cause there ain't nothin in the world like a —
Here I go,

Now hit me!
Hit me twice!
Hit me three times!

I do the Monkey,
The Mashed Potatoes.
I do the Jerk.
Now watch me work. Ow!

(He dances)

You can look up and down
All over town.
Ask anybody
Ask all around.
Who knows the grooves?
Who busta' moves?
I got the...
And the...
And the...

HORSE & JERRY

I'm/he's what your sister and your mama's
Always thinking of.
I/He take(s) up eight whole chapters in the book of love.
It's a long, low load with a deep, dark tan.
There ain't nothing in the world like a big black man.

HORSE

Sing!

HORSE & JERRY

A big black man.

HORSE

(To **DAVE**)
Help me out, big guy.

JERRY & DAVE

A big black man.

HORSE

(To **MALCOLM**)
Your turn, pretty boy.

JERRY, DAVE & MALCOLM

A big black man.

HORSE

(*To* HAROLD)
What you got, Mr. Four Eyes?

JERRY, DAVE & MALCOLM	HAROLD
A big black man	*Gotta love a big black man.*
A big black man	*Gotta love a big black man.*
A big black man	*Gotta love a big black man.*

ALL

A big black man!

JERRY

You're hired.

(HORSE *ends with a whoop and an impressive,
though only partially successful, split*)

TRANSITION

(*A spot hits* ETHAN, *all smiles, all eager like a puppy to audition.* HAROLD *is hiding behind his newspaper*)

ETHAN

Hi, I'm Ethan Girard. Some of you look familiar from the plant.
I guess things are tough for all of us.

HAROLD

(*Whispered, behind the newspaper*)
I've seen him before. He plastered our bathroom. He knows me.
Get rid of him, he'll blow my cover.

TERRENCE MCNALLY & DAVID YAZBEK

JERRY

Keep your head down, you'll be fine. What are you going to do for us, Mr. Girard?

ETHAN

It's Ethan, please. I've always wanted to be a dancer but I couldn't dance. My favorite movie is *Singin' In The Rain*. Donald O'Connor does that running up the wall thing, which isn't really dancing, which is why I thought maybe I could do it.

JERRY

What running up the wall thing?

ETHAN

I'm Donald O'Connor, you're you. Watch. Here goes nothing.

(*He runs towards the proscenium and manages to get two feet on the wall for a brief moment before crashing heavily to the floor*)

JEANETTE

That's a show-stopper.

MALCOLM

Are you all right?

ETHAN
(*Cheerfully, getting back on his feet*)
I didn't get enough speed. Let me try again. I know I can do it. I'll yell when I am ready.

(*This time he goes off-stage*)

MALCOLM

Hey, has anybody seen Davie today?

JERRY

His wife is on him to take one of those security jobs at Wal-Mart. I wouldn't be surprised if he went to those interviews they're having.

ETHAN

(*Off*)
I'm ready!

(*This time* ETHAN *streaks across the stage
at great speed and vanishes behind the
opposite proscenium. There is a great crash
from off-stage.* MALCOLM *hurries off*)

JEANETTE

Anybody gonna call 911?

(MALCOLM *brings* ETHAN *back on*)

ETHAN

It's better in the movie but I think I can nail it next time.

JERRY

That's fine, Ethan.

ETHAN

I can do it at home. These are funny walls.

JERRY

That won't be necessary. So. You don't sing.

ETHAN

(*Always cheerful*)
No.

JERRY

You don't dance.

ETHAN

No.

JERRY

I hope you don't take this the wrong way but what the hell do you do?

ETHAN

Well, I thought maybe this.

> (*He pulls the belt out of his trousers and pulls them down in one movement. The faces on the Gang — a mixture of awe, shock and respect — tell us what ETHAN'S unique talent is/are*)

JEANETTE

Gentlemen, put on your sunglasses. We suddenly have a lot of glimmer.

HAROLD

> (*Lowering his newspaper*)

Jesus, Mary and Joseph!

ETHAN

Oh hello, Mr. Nichols, I didn't see you there. I plastered his bathroom.

HAROLD

Hello, Ethan.

> (*NATHAN, too, is transfixed. JERRY suddenly remembers his son is there*)

JERRY

Nathan! Close your eyes!

> (*He puts his hand over NATHAN'S eyes*)

ETHAN

Is there anything else you want to see?

MEN

No!!!

TRANSITION

(Lights come up on DAVE, in his
underwear, sitting on the edge of his bed)

SONG: *YOU RULE MY WORLD*

DAVE

Look at you. You're lying there.
I feel your milky skin, caress your silky hair.
For all these years you've been with me,
I tilt my chin and what I see is
Only you...

Not feet or knees.
You grumble and I stumble towards the Muenster cheese.
I'm in your spell, a chubby fool,
And anyone can tell
You rule my world — my world —
No matter what I do
You rule my world.

GEORGIE

What's the matter, Dave?

DAVE

I can't sleep.

GEORGIE

Come to think of it, neither can I, Big Man.

(She runs a finger across his bare shoulders)

DAVE

Don't. I'm beat.

(Attempt at a joke)

You have no idea how exhausting unemployment is.

GEORGIE

You'll find work. They're still hiring at Wal-Mart. Security guards, stock boys, cashiers even.

DAVE

It's woman's work.

GEORGIE

Well, whatever makes you happy, David.

(*GEORGIE, pained, removes her arm, turns away from DAVE.*

Lights come up on HAROLD and VICKI in bed)

VICKI

Guess what I'm gonna dream about? Those two weeks in Puerto Rico you promised me. Good night, Harold.

SONG: YOU RULE MY WORLD (PART II)

HAROLD

Look at you — My life, my dream —
My lady with the eighty dollar slumber cream,
The hundred dollar haircuts,
The novelty appliances we never use.

And all those shoes
You bought for when we go on the Alaskan Cruise.
My boat is sinking, I don't care.
You're everything I want,
You rule my world — my world —
You're everything I need.

DAVE

Anywhere you go I'll follow.

HAROLD

Anywhere I'll follow you.

DAVE

Anything you want, I'll give you.

HAROLD

Anything at all.

HAROLD & DAVE

Anytime you feel hollow, don't worry.

DAVE

I'll swallow it whole.

HAROLD

I'll make you whole.
Look at me.

DAVE

Just take a look at me.

HAROLD

And hold me hard.

DAVE

You never leave my side.

HAROLD

A moment please, before they seize the Visa card!

DAVE

Why can't I let you go?

HAROLD

'Cause I'd do anything to keep you.

DAVE

Why can't I just lose —

HAROLD & DAVE

You rule my world, my world.

TERRENCE MCNALLY & DAVID YAZBEK

DAVE

Though I'm unemployed,

HAROLD

A tad depressed,

DAVE

I'm overweight,

HAROLD

I'm overdressed,

HAROLD & DAVE

There's nothing I can do, you rule my world.

DAVE

There's nothing I can do.

TRANSITION

> *(We are back at the mill. JERRY is practicing some strip movements. NATHAN is watching him)*

JERRY

What are you looking at? The guys are gonna be here any minute. It's our first rehearsal. I wanna look good. Now, is it better when I do this? Or when I do this?

NATHAN

It's better if you just don't.

JERRY

Hey, c'mon, Nath, if I'm gonna pull this off I need all the confidence I can get. In two weeks I'm going to be standing in front of a thousand women without my clothes on. Should I go to a gym?

NATHAN

I don't know. Ask Estelle.

JERRY

What is that supposed to mean?

NATHAN

She's the expert. "Oooo! Aaaahh! Do it Jerry."

JERRY

All right, that's it, no more sleep-overs.

NATHAN

Who for? Me or Estelle?

JERRY

Both of you! I'm not doing this for a laugh, you know. I'm doing this for you and your fucking maintenance.

NATHAN

I gotta go.

(*NATHAN starts off*)

JERRY

I didn't mean it like that, Nath, you know I didn't mean it like that. So you and me can keep seeing each other. They want to take you away from me. It's not gonna happen. I told Teddy, "Don't hold your breath. He's my kid and I'm gonna keep him."

NATHAN

Teddy's okay.

JERRY

You like him?

NATHAN
Yeah, and he's nice to mom.

JERRY
You know he wants to marry her?

NATHAN
I told her she should.

JERRY
What did she say?

NATHAN
She said she was thinking about it. I gotta go. Teddy bought hockey tickets.

JERRY
(He has trouble saying this)
I like you. You're a great kid. Hell, I love you. You're my son and I'm not going to lose you.

(He'll say it. What the hell?)

I think you're supposed to say something back, Nath.

(He cuffs NATHAN gently on the shoulder. NATHAN cuffs him back. JERRY returns it a bit harder and NATHAN really lets him have it on the shoulder. JERRY gathers him into a tight hug)

NATHAN
I love you, too, but it's gonna be a really great game. Have a good rehearsal.

(He goes as DAVE enters)

JERRY
Twelve years old going on forty.

DAVE

(*Meaning JERRY*)
Thirty-two going on ten.

JERRY

I still need a sixth man, Dave.

DAVE

A fat bastard like me? No way, Jer. Besides, I told Georgie I'd check out this security job at the mall.

JERRY

Those Chippendales aren't checking anything out. Raking it in, they are. Fifty thousand dollars!

DAVE

God, what I couldn't do with that kind of money. Season tickets for the Bills and something nice for Georgie.

JERRY

Yeah, a new vacuum cleaner.

DAVE

No, but a new roof.

JERRY

What's stopping you?

DAVE

Common sense.

JERRY

When have we ever listened to common sense? Think of Georgie's face when she sees you up there on that stage with the music and the lights and all those women screaming for you and you looking like...

DAVE

Refrigerator Perry.

JERRY

No! There you go again, negative! Like, like John Travolta.

DAVE

Really? John Travolta? Georgie loves John Travolta. I could really be like that?

JERRY

With the right light and moves, you're gonna be better than John Travolta.

DAVE

Fuck it, I'm in. Eat your hearts out, ladies!

JERRY

We got our sixth man, fellas!

(*All the Gang, six strong now with the addition of ETHAN, MALCOLM, HAROLD and HORSE, are arriving and getting ready to rehearse. JEANETTE busies herself at the piano*)

JEANETTE

Take a deep breath. The smell of fear. There's nothing like the first day of rehearsals.

HAROLD

Who's going to be keeping that one on a leash?

MALCOLM

She's the only pro here, Harold.

JEANETTE

Nobody try any funny stuff and we'll get along fine. Arthur Godfrey came on to me once and almost did not live to tell the tale.

HAROLD

Let's get to work.

(The men are all lined up now—a scruffy, disparate lot.
HAROLD has his work cut out for him)

HAROLD
All right. Now. So. Let's start at the very beginning.

ETHAN & MALCOLM
"A very good place to start."

(ETHAN and MALCOLM, startled, look at each other)

ETHAN
The Sound of Music?

MALCOLM
It's my favorite movie.

ETHAN
Mine, too. I've seen it about two hundred times.

MALCOLM
Try *three*!

HAROLD
Gentlemen! And....! Starting with our right foot, five, six, follow me.

(He nods to JEANETTE, who pounds
out a rhythmic accompaniment on her old piano)

Seven, eight! Right and right. Left and left.

(HAROLD steps out. The other men just look at him)

Gentlemen, you gotta work with me. Again! Horse, I need you to
anchor me down at the end. Jeanette, from the top. Just listen to the
music. Let your body do the rest. Think of *Saturday Night Fever*.

(MALCOLM has struck that movie's iconic pose)

Forget *Saturday Night Fever*. Just be yourselves. Five, six, seven, eight, right and right, left and left. No, I need you to step forward and you to go back. Horse, you're killing me.

(*JEANETTE starts to play. The men's new enthusiasm does not translate itself into anything resembling a coherent line of Chippendale dancers*)

HAROLD
No, no, no. You stay put. And you come forward. Again. Stop!

MALCOLM
Sorry.

HAROLD
Jesus, you don't have to be Einstein to remember these steps. I've seen you guys play basketball. You remember those plays.

DAVE
Those aren't real plays; we're just having fun.

MALCOLM
Basketball's natural. This stuff is weird.

ETHAN
When you're shooting hoops, who's listening to music? You just move where you gotta move.

JEANETTE
I can't play any slower.

HAROLD
This is a disaster.

JERRY
Wait a minute, wait a minute. You're on to something, Harold. I think what Harold means gentlemen, is sort of Michael Jordan combination. Fake, spin, shoot.

(The other men instantly know what he's talking about)

ETHAN, HORSE, MALCOLM, HAROLD & DAVE
Fake, spin, shoot.

SONG: MICHAEL JORDAN'S BALL

JERRY
When Michael's got the basketball
It's Michael's house from wall to wall.
You hear that name, it's a diff'rent game
When it's Michael Jordan's ball.

When it's Michael's ball, you're dead, you're through,
'Cause Michael takes the game to you.
He's in your face, you lost the race.
It's Michael Jordan's ball.

The fake, the spin, the drive and then he's in the paint.
The pump, the jump, and he's up in the air like a Goddamn saint!

When Michael bolts and he penetrates
You feel the volts he generates.
He's slick as soap, he's king, he's Pope,
He's Michael Friggin' Jordan!

JERRY & MEN
You fake, you spin, you drive, and then you're in the paint.
You pump, jump, and you're up there! You're up there!
You're up there! You're up there! You're up there!
You're up there! You're up there! You're up there!

And you're through the roof, you're in the zone.
Two-hundred-proof testosterone.
You're bad, you're hot, you're almost God!

JERRY

You're Michael Jordan!

Say it!

I'm Michael —

HORSE

I'm Michael —

ETHAN

I'm Michael —

MALCOLM

I'm Michael —

HAROLD

I'm Michael —

DAVE

I'm Michael —

JERRY, MALCOLM & DAVE	**HAROLD, HORSE & ETHAN**
I'm Michael —	*Michael Jordan*
I'm Michael —	*Michael Jordan*
I'm Michael —	*Michael Jordan*
I'm Michael —	*Michael Jordan*
I'm Michael —	*Michael Jordan*
I'm Michael —	*Michael Jordan*

DAVE

Let's get ready to rumba!!

> *(Lots of high-fives. We've come a very long way in a very few minutes)*

(JEANETTE pounds it out. The men take a tentative step. The curtain is falling)

END OF ACT ONE

Above: The women perform "The Goods."

Left to right: Jerry (Patrick Wilson), Dave (John Ellison Conlee), and Malcolm (Jason Danieley) sing "Big-Ass Rock."

Left to right: Malcolm (Jason Danieley), Ethan (Romain Frugé), Dave (John Ellison Conlee), Jerry (Patrick Wilson), Horse (André De Shields), and Harold (Marcus Neville) sing "Let It Go."

Right: Jerry (Patrick Wilson) sings "Man."

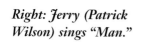

Left: Horse (André De Shields) performs "Big Black Man."

Left to right: Jerry (Patrick Wilson), Dave (John Ellison Conlee), and Buddy "Keno" Walsh (Denis Jones).

Left to right: Ethan (Romain Frugé), Jerry (Patrick Wilson), and Malcolm (Jason Danieley) sing "Michael Jordan's Ball."

Below: The guys perform "Michael Jordan's Ball."

Left: Kathleen Freeman as Jeanette Burmeister.

Right: John Ellison Conlee as Dave Bukatinsky and Patrick Wilson as Jerry Lukowski.

Father and son: Nicholas Cutro as Nathan Lukowski and Patrick Wilson as Jerry Lukowski..

Clockwise from bottom: Ethan (Romain Frugé), Dave (John Ellison Conlee), Harold (Marcus Neville), Malcolm (Jason Danieley), and Horse (André De Shields) perform "The Goods."

ACT TWO

The factory. One week later. Gloom and despair. The men look utterly defeated. You could cut the sense of defeat in the room with a knife.

They have just finished an especially bad rehearsal.

JEANETTE picks out a mournful blues on her piano. No one pays it much attention.

Nor do they seem to notice ETHAN, who is determined to do his Donald O'Connor thing. He hurls himself at the wall with a fury and determination that are cheerful and demonic at one and the same time.

JEANETTE
That guy with the bullwhip is starting to look good to me. Once more from the top, Harold? I didn't think so.

ETHAN
Harold, I think I've got it this time.

JERRY
They laughed at Columbus. They laughed at the Wright Brothers.

HORSE
And now they're gonna be laughing at us.

JERRY
We just need more practice. It's only been a week.

HAROLD
It's my fault, boys.

DAVE
It's nobody's fault.

HAROLD

I've let you down. I'm not a teacher. I can't even get you in a fucking straight line. Sorry, Jeanette.

JEANETTE

For what?

HAROLD

Skip it.

JEANETTE

Anybody want a hit? No? Jesus, this is like working with Lawrence Welk.

ETHAN

Are you watching?

> (*He hurls himself at the wall. This time he doesn't get up*)

JEANETTE

You gotta love that kid.

SONG: *JEANETTE'S NUMBER*

JEANETTE

This gig's an echo of that time with Buddy Greco
When we did the Desert Inn in '59.
The dancing girls were clunky
The drummer was a junkie.
But we pulled the act together
And we killed 'em every time.

That having been said, frankly,
I think that things are worse here.

> (*ETHAN crashes to the floor again*)

That guy and his head are gonna need some kind of nurse here.
It's like a friggin' curse here.

Things could be better.

So sue me. It's the truth.

Things could be better 'round here.

It's an attitude problem. Seen it a million times.

I was subbing with Stan Kenton
In this seedy club in Trenton
When I heard my third divorce had just gone through.
I coulda torn my heart out,
But instead I got my chart out
And I gave 'em all a lesson in the way to play the blues.

That having been said,
Something is even more morose here.
Just looking ahead's making me feel real gross here.
We aren't even close here.

Things could be better.

Could they get any worse? I don't think so!

Things could be better 'round here.

It's like a putz museum
A showbiz mausoleum.
Things could be better 'round here.

DAVE
There's a problem with the timing.

HORSE
There's a problem with the groove.

HAROLD
There's an overwhelming lethargy nothing can improve.

JEANETTE
You can sense defeat get closer every time they add a move...

(***ETHAN*** *crashes to the floor*)

MALCOLM	**ETHAN**
There's only six days.	*Where am I? Don't worry.*

JERRY/HAROLD/HORSE/DAVE	**ETHAN**
There's only six days.	*I'll get it. Who are you?*

JEANETTE
This guy needs a helmet.
That guy needs some lipo.
And I could use some Geritol delivered in a hypo.
But I don't wanna gripe —

MEN
Oh — things could be better.

JEANETTE
You bet your ass they could!

Things could be better 'round here.

JEANETTE
Now let me tell you something...

> *I've played for hoofers who can't hoof,*
> *I've played for tone deaf singers.*

And once, when I insulted Frank
I played with broken fingers.

I've paid my dues,
I know the blues,
Of this I can assure you.
So now I'll say it one last time
'Cause I don't want to bore you.
I've got some bad news for you —

JEANETTE	MEN
Things could be better.	*Things could be better.*
	They really could be better.

JEANETTE
Let's face it. We suck!

MEN
We're deep down in the ditch, man.

JEANETTE
This showbiz is a bitch, man.
Things could be better.

MEN
We could be better.

JEANETTE
Things could be better 'round—

JEANETTE
You know what Kate Smith used to say about a bad rehearsal?
"Usually means a bad performance."

…here.

JERRY
We'll be the laughing stock of Buffalo if we chicken out now.

MALCOLM

We'll be the laughing stock of Buffalo if we don't. Ethan's gonna end up with brain damage.

ETHAN

I just need more time, guys.

JERRY

That's the spirit, Ethan. They always laugh when people say they're gonna go where no one's gone before. And when they get there, it's nothing but R-E-S-P-E-C-T.

(*He explodes in a fury of steps*)

HORSE

Somebody's been practicing!

JERRY

Now come on, are we men or mice?

(*JEANETTE starts up at the piano as the men get in line.
General enthusiasm from all but HAROLD*)

HAROLD

(*Music under*)
Okay, now let's give the ladies what they came for. First, the belt.

MEN

The belt...

HAROLD

We verrryy slooowly unbuckle and...wham!

(*He pulls his belt off with one dramatic gesture.
When DAVE repeats it, he practically puts ETHAN'S eye out*)

DAVE

Wham! Sorry.

MALCOLM

You all right, Eth?

(The dance comes to a halt)

HAROLD

Maybe we were a little premature. From the top, Jeanette, nice and slow this time.

JERRY

May I be excused, teach?

DAVE

What's up?

JERRY

Tony Giordano wants an advance in case we don't show Sunday night. No way, I told him, we'll show.

HORSE

How much does he want?

JERRY

A thousand dollars.

MALCOLM

A thousand dollars. Where are we gonna get that kind of money?

JERRY

Leave it to me. It's a done deal. Work on your pelvic thrusts and lay off the cheeseburgers. Nathan!

TRANSITION

> *(The men continue to dance as we begin*
> *to hear the sounds of PAM'S workplace.*
> *We are in the cafeteria. PAM enters.*

She sees JERRY and NATHAN gesturing to her.
She goes over to them and ruffles NATHAN'S hair)

PAM

Hi, honey. I've been telling the girls how big you're getting. This is him, ladies!

WOMEN

Hi!

PAM

(To JERRY)
Hello, Jerry. This is a surprise.

JERRY

A nice one, I hope.

PAM

That depends on you. I want us to be friends.

(*An attractive young woman, also a factory worker, crosses. It's ESTELLE*)

ESTELLE

Hi, Jerry. Hi, Nathan. What do you think of your old man now?

PAM

I still need those invoices, Estelle.

ESTELLE

I only have two legs, Mrs. Lukowski.

PAM

That's not what I heard.

ESTELLE

We're all holding our breath 'til Sunday.

PAM

(*To* *JERRY*)
What was that all about?

JERRY

Nothing much. You know Estelle. Nathan, go get yourself a Coke.

NATHAN

I don't —

PAM

Here, honey.

(*She gives him a coin.* *NATHAN* *goes*)

He looks more like you every day. He's gonna be a real heart-breaker.

JERRY

Thanks.

PAM

It wasn't a compliment.

JERRY

Ouch! So, how are you? You look good.

PAM

Jerry, I look the same as I did last week. Is this about Nathan?

JERRY

In a way. Remember on our honeymoon, we were on that boat at the falls, Maid of the Mist, and I promised you I was going to amount to something, something you and our kids were gonna be proud of?

PAM

Jerry, I was proud of you when I married you.

JERRY

I know I've let a lot of people down since then, mainly you and Nathan, but that's about to change.

PAM

You got a job? That's wonderful, Jerry. A man with your potential! Where? Out at the mall?

JERRY

It's not a job per se. It's more like a special engagement sort of thing. But listen, I'm going to get all your money for you, our money, Nathan's, oh you know what I mean. I hate it when you look at me like that.

PAM

Go on.

JERRY

The thing is, Pam, you have to invest a little to get something back.

PAM

No. I don't believe this. You're hustling me for money.

JERRY

I'll pay you back, don't you trust me?

PAM

Jerry, do you know how much you already owe me?

JERRY

That's different. This is for Nathan.

PAM

You want to go on being his father? Then you better start acting like one.

JERRY

What do you think I'm doing?

PAM

You want some money? I need someone in packing, right now. Nine-fifty an hour.

JERRY

I can't.

PAM

Why not?

JERRY

I can't tell you.

PAM

Grow up, Jerry. This isn't a game. He's our son but you're gonna lose him. Don't make me do this to you. I'm not the enemy.

(PAM goes. ESTELLE comes over to him)

ESTELLE

What a bitch!

JERRY

Shut up, Estelle.

(JERRY goes)

ESTELLE

What did I say? Isn't that what you're always telling me? When are you coming over? Goddamn men, you're more trouble than you're worth.

TRANSITION

(MALCOLM'S house. He's practicing his belt moves. He accidentally releases the belt and it goes flying offstage)

TRANSITION

(JERRY'S house. He's on the phone)

JERRY

You'll get your money, Tony. I just need a little more time. My usual sources dried up on me.

(NATHAN enters. He's dressed for bed)

Can I call you back? My kid's staying over.

(He hangs up)

The good news is your old man isn't going to be embarrassing you Sunday night. The bad news is we're not going to be seeing so much of each other.

(NATHAN hands him an envelope)

What's this?

NATHAN

Open it.

JERRY

Nathan, I can't take this. It's your savings.

NATHAN

It's the thousand dollars you need for the club.

JERRY

It's for when you're eighteen, when you'll need it for college.

NATHAN

You told mom you'd get it back.

JERRY

I know, but you don't want to start listening to what I say.

NATHAN

You *said* so. That's good enough for me.

JERRY

Jesus, Nath!

(*He pulls him to him and holds him close*)

NATHAN

Don't forget, that's my college. 'Night, Dad.

(*NATHAN lies down on the hideaway bed and gets ready to sleep. JERRY stands looking down at him*)

SONG: BREEZE OFF THE RIVER

JERRY

There's a breeze off the river
Through the crack in the window pane.
There's my boy on the pillow
And I feel like I'm lost again.

Everybody knows the secret.
They all know what their life should be
And they move like a river.
Everybody knows except for me.

And I never feel like somebody somebody calls a father.
I can't explain
But when I look at you, kid, it's like a mirror.
It spins my head. It wakes me

Like the breeze off the river,
Every time I see your face.
And it's strange but familiar —
Like a map of a better place.

And sometimes I feel like I live in a shadow
And shadow's all I see,

Then you jump straight up and you grab the moon
And you make it shine on me.
Where do you get it from?

Everybody knows the secret.
Well I don't and I never did.
I don't know any secret.
All I know is I love you, kid.
All I know is I love you, kid.
All I know...

TRANSITION

(**HAROLD'S** *house, the living room. The Gang is all there*)

HAROLD
We've only got a couple of hours before she's back.

(*The others are busy checking their new rehearsal digs out*)

MALCOLM
Looks like real gold.

HAROLD
Put that down, you'll break it!

HORSE
Very la-tee-da, Harold.

ETHAN
These are the kind of walls I was talking about.

HAROLD
Don't even think about it.

DAVE
You got a beer?

TERRENCE MCNALLY & DAVID YAZBEK

HAROLD

No. I must be insane to let you rehearse here.

MALCOLM

You didn't have much choice. Who knew they'd hired another security guard? We're lucky we didn't get caught.

JERRY

Okay, gentlemen, D-Day, this is it. Today we take our clothes off.

(This announcement is met with 0% enthusiasm)

HORSE

Do we have to?

JERRY

Oh, come on! If we can't take our clothes off in front of each other, how are we gonna do it in front of a thousand women?

DAVE

All of them?

JERRY

Yes, all of them. When did everybody get so modest? Just pretend you're in a locker room.

JERRY

(Very jock)
"Yo, Bukatinsky, how's it hanging?" Let me re-phrase that.

HAROLD

Just a minute. This is a nice neighborhood in case you haven't noticed.

(JERRY is unstoppable now.
HAROLD is still closing the curtains)

JERRY

Shirts off.

DAVE

No looking and no laughing, you bastards.

(*Keeping their eyes very much to themselves,
everyone begins to take off their shirt*)

JERRY

Suck your stomach in, Dave.

DAVE

I am.

JERRY

Sorry.

HORSE

What are you looking at?

ETHAN

Nothing, nothing.

HORSE

Well don't.

MALCOLM

It's a birthmark. I've had it since birth.

HAROLD

I used to have a real job.

(*They all have their shirts off now*)

JERRY

That wasn't so hard, was it?

HAROLD

Speak for yourself.

TERRENCE MCNALLY & DAVID YAZBEK

JERRY

One small step for a man; one enormous step for *Hot Metal*.

ETHAN

What's *Hot Metal*?

JERRY

We are. Nathan came up with it. And now our pants. Gentlemen, the day of reckoning has come.

HORSE

(*In his own private misery*)
You can say that again.

> (*They take their trousers off. The variety of underwear is astonishing. HORSE'S is especially big and baggy, which does not go unnoticed*)

JERRY

Horse by name, horse by nature, huh, Horse?

HORSE

Shut up, will you!

JERRY

Times like this, I wish I was a black man, you know what I mean, Horse?

HORSE

Not really. I want you guys to start calling me Noah now.

ETHAN

Sure thing, Horse.

HORSE

Horse is a nickname. I'm too old for a nickname.

ETHAN

(*Ready to strip*)
You want us to take our shorts off?

(*His are practically down*)

HORSE

Not so fast!

JERRY

Horse is right. What's your hurry? Savor the moment. Feel good about yourself.

(*They move around a bit, very self-consciously, in their underwear*)

ETHAN

How come you're so brown, Harold?

HAROLD

I don't know.

ETHAN

Somebody's got a sunbed!

(*Whistles and coy noises from the Gang*)

HAROLD

It's Vicki's and no, you can't use it, so don't even think about asking. It's not paid for.

JERRY

Anti-wrinkle cream. Do you think it works on men?

HAROLD

It hasn't worked on Vicki. Put it down, I said.

DAVE

What am I supposed to do with this?

　　　　　TERRENCE MCNALLY & DAVID YAZBEK

(He stares sorrowfully down at his stomach)

JERRY
It's not too bad from the front. Just don't turn sideways.

HORSE
My Aunt Claudia has a weight problem. She wraps herself in Saran Wrap, Dave.

DAVE
Saran Wrap? I'm not a drumstick. Saran Wrap yourself.

HAROLD
Fat, David, is a feminist issue.

DAVE
What is that supposed to mean if you're a man?

HAROLD
It's supposed to mean that fat or thin, you're beautiful.

DAVE
Do you believe that?

HAROLD
No, and I don't know anyone who does. You are what you look like. Ask Vicki.

(He picks up one of VICKI'S fashion magazines)

This is what we're all supposed to look like, men and women.

JERRY
Holy Mary Mother of God! Dave, look at this, it's better than Playboy.

HAROLD
But who looks like that? Tell me, who?

JERRY

This one does!

HAROLD

She's a picture in a magazine!

JERRY

That's good enough for me.

SONG: THE GOODS

JERRY

Take a look at this girl. That's everything I like.
She got the face, she got the waist, she got the legs.

MALCOLM

Naw, her tits are too big.

JERRY

What are you, crazy?

Bodacious fun-bags are a must!
They gotta be C or D or better.
They gotta pose a threat to the sweater. Ow!

She got the goods.
That's an eight or nine at least!
She got the goods.

HORSE

Let me see that.

(Glances at magazine. Shakes his head)

Mm-mm. She has some irredeemable flaws. I give her a six.

(Leafs through magazine)

Ah—now there's a ten!

JERRY

You call that a ten?

HORSE

Based on the booty.

ETHAN

What do you mean? It's huge.

HORSE

She got a butt like a battleship!
I don't need to look above the hip.

She got that *shelf* kinda ass. You could display your tchotchkes, your collectibles on there.

Baby got back. That's a fact.
You could park a wide track Pontiac in that crack.

Now that's the goods.

"The bigger the cushion—"

JERRY

She's got a sofa-bed back there!

DAVE

Well we just better hope the women are more forgiving than we are.

HORSE

What is that supposed to mean?

DAVE

If they're looking at us Saturday night the way we're usually looking at them — well, we're in trouble. He just said her tits were too big. They might say the same thing about your dick.

JERRY

I can deal with that. Is there a bathroom?

(*He exits*)

DAVE

I'm being serious!

MALCOLM

It's different...

(*Shrugging*)

...we're men. They wouldn't do that to us, would they?

(*The* WOMEN *appear in the* MEN'S *fantasy as their (and every man's) worst nightmare*)

GEORGIE

Take a look at that Opie-looking jerk with the pigeon chest!

PAM

And I give that fat guy's ass a two, but I wish I had such voluptuous breasts.

VICKI

And what about old Father Time over there?
Yea, sure he can dance.
But I didn't pay fifty bucks to look at
Red Foxx skip around in a pair of blue underpants.

WOMEN

This ain't the goods.

DAVE

What happens when they say that?

WOMEN

This is not the goods!

TERRENCE MCNALLY & DAVID YAZBEK

(They cackle)

DAVE

Maybe they'll say you have saggy tits.

MALCOLM

I do not have saggy tits. And I wasn't talking about her personality. She's probably a very nice woman.

DAVE

She's not going to be talking about your personality either when you're standing up there in all your masculine glory — which is lucky for you 'cause you're basically a bastard.

(Points at himself)

And I tell you, guys, anti-wrinkle cream there may be but anti-fat-bastard cream there ain't.

ESTELLE

(Indicating individual men)
He's fat, he's old, he's skinny, he's bald, he's short,
He's got pimples on his ass…

ESTELLE, PAM, & VICKI

He's fat, he's old, he's skinny, he's bald, he's short,
He's got pimples on his ass…

WOMEN

He's fat, he's old, he's skinny, he's bald, he's short,
He's got pimples on his ass
He's fat, he's old, he's skinny, he's —

MEN

Women can be lovers.
Women can be pals.
Women can be modern types
Or sweet old fashioned gals.

Women can be angels on earth
But then again,
Holy Goddamn fucking shit

WOMEN

Talk about butt ugly!

MEN

Women can be men.

WOMEN

He's fat, he's old, he's skinny, he's bald, he's short,
He's fat, he's old, he's skinny, he's bald, he's short.

HAROLD	**WOMEN**
I've got pimples	*He's got pimples*
All over my ass!!!	*All over his ass.*

Look at it! Jesus!

That ain't the goods.   *That ain't the goods.*

HORSE
I feel extremely insecure
All of a sudden.

That ain't the goods.

DAVE
What am I doin' here?
What am I doin' here?

That ain't the goods.

ALL MEN
What am I doing here?
Why the hell am I here?
That ain't the goods. *What the hell am I*
doing here?
That ain't the goods. *This ain't the goods.*

This ain't the goods. *This ain't the goods.*

TERRENCE MCNALLY & DAVID YAZBEK

ALL

That (this) ain't the goods.

(JERRY returns carrying a brown paper bag)

JERRY

(*Entering*)
This is probably not the best time for this but...

*(He reaches in his bag and produces a handful
of bright red leather G-strings. The Gang
examines them with a mixture of awe and terror)*

DAVE

Oh, Mother of God!

JERRY

I told them we wanted something sexy.

HORSE

This isn't sexy. This is naked.

HAROLD

It doesn't look very sexy to me.

JERRY

Well not when you hold it like that — like it's gonna bite. They'll be sexy when we're in 'em. They're top of the line. Genuine leather almost.

DAVE

How much?

JERRY

Twenty-five each.

MALCOLM

You don't get much for your money, do you?

(The doorbell rings. Panic)

HAROLD
Hide!

MEN
Where?

HAROLD
In there.

*(HAROLD wraps something around his
waist. The other men go. HAROLD goes
to door and opens it. Two REPO MEN storm in)*

HAROLD
Now just a minute.

REPO MAN #1
I've got a repossess order for one Sony Trinitron 42-inch TV and
a Westinghouse sunbed.

HAROLD
We only owe another four hundred on the sunbed.

REPO MAN #2
They're not worth that much second-hand.

HAROLD
They're not second-hand.

REPO MAN #1
They are now, mac.

(They've already picked up the TV)

Now where's the sunbed?

(The Gang appears in their underwear.
DAVE leads them, terribly impressive in all his
big-bellied splendor. The REPO MEN look terrified)

REPO MAN #2

What the hell?

DAVE

Put it down and fuck off.

(He takes a step towards the two REPO MEN,
who drop the TV and fly out the door)

That's telling 'em! A man's home is his castle, am I right?

MEN

Now that's the goods!

(They congratulate themselves. This
stripping is gonna be all right!)

JERRY

Gentlemen, dress rehearsal, Thursday.

TRANSITION

(The Gang disperses in high spirits. We follow
DAVE home. His spirits visibly wilt as he
thinks about Sunday night.

Soon he is in the bathroom, the door locked.
He is morosely wrapping himself with
Saran Wrap, then sits eating a bag of potato chips.

GEORGIE knocks softly. She is dressed for bed)

GEORGIE

Dave? Dave...you said you were coming back. We can have a good cuddle, that's all. We don't have to...what's up, big man, huh? Dave, you gotta talk with me. I'm your wife.

(*DAVE pulls the Saran Wrap off with a violent gesture. He takes a big bite of a candy bar. He stands up and opens the door*)

DAVE

Are they still hiring security men at the mall?

TRANSITION

(*The factory. Dress rehearsal. ETHAN enters and hangs up a make-shift curtain. HORSE enters. He is practicing his dance moves*)

HORSE

It ain't working, Lord, it ain't getting any bigger. What am I gonna do? Today's our dress rehearsal. Our undress rehearsal.

(*He paces and frets as the others warm up backstage*)

HAROLD

Where are they? It's bad form to keep an audience waiting. I hate it when it happens to me.

ETHAN

We can't start without Dave.

MALCOLM

Jerry is getting him. He must have forgotten the dress rehearsal.

JEANETTE

Anything the matter, Horse?

TERRENCE MCNALLY & DAVID YAZBEK

HORSE
That is. My nickname. I'm not a Horse. They're all expecting me to overwhelm everybody with the size of my...I'm sorry, Jeanette, I can't use words like penis or Johnson in front of a lady. It's my upbringing.

JEANETTE
I appreciate that. So you're trying to tell me you've got a small dick, Horse?

HORSE
I'm telling you no such thing! I'm average.

JEANETTE
Most men are. That's why it's called average. Let me look: I'll tell you if you're average or not.

HORSE
Are you crazy, woman?

JEANETTE
No, but I've been married eight times, so I guess I know what average is. Now quit worrying. Come the moment of truth, nobody's gonna be thinking of anybody's size but his own. Besides, they didn't hire you because you were big. They hired you because you were good.

HORSE
Thank you, Jeanette. Sometimes you need to hear something like that. It's not easy being a big black man.

JEANETTE
You're gonna show these boys it's not a man's size but what he does with it that matters.

HORSE
Woman, where have you been all my life?

(*He hugs her hard*)

NATHAN

I can't hold them much longer.

MALCOLM

They're all so old, Nathan.

NATHAN

Of course they're old. They're from the rest home. They're on an outing.

JEANETTE

Senior citizens can be a great audience. Of course they can turn on you, too. Look what they did to Eddie Fisher. It's bad luck to peek, Mr. Simmons.

HORSE

You got my aunt out there!

NATHAN

I didn't know she was your aunt.

(*JERRY enters*)

JERRY

Everybody ready? Let's do it.

ETHAN

What happened? Where's Dave?

JERRY

He's not coming. He's taking that security job at Wal-Mart. I knew he was a loser.

(*He quickly starts to change*)

NATHAN

Dave's your best friend.

JERRY
Was, Nath, was. Let's get going. Jeanette!

JEANETTE
I don't know why I'm nervous. Who's gonna be looking at me?

(She goes through the curtain)

JERRY
We who are about to die salute you!

(JERRY comes out to meet their audience)

JERRY
Ladies, welcome to the dress rehearsal of *Hot Metal*. When you talk about this back at the nursing home, and we certainly hope you will, remember to tell your friends we'll be appearing this Sunday for one performance only at Tony Giordano's place over on Route 11. Ladies, without further ado, I give you *Hot Metal*.

TRANSITION

(The Gang appear in their security guard outfits and begin to dance. It is the first time we have seen them as a group since their earliest rehearsals. They've made a quantum leap. They're almost credible as male dancers.

Their small audience is appreciative. NATHAN mimics their movements from his place by JEANETTE.

Pretty soon the joint is jumping. As the music gets louder and louder and the celebration gets merrier, all are oblivious to the sound of sirens.

Suddenly all the lights are turned on. The men are caught mid-bump and grind)

POLICE SERGEANT

Nobody move! You're under arrest! All of you!

> (*Panic. Only MALCOLM and ETHAN are quick
> enough to run, clad only in their red leather G-strings*)

TRANSITION

> (*MALCOLM's room. MALCOLM climbs
> in through a window. A pair of hands
> appear on the sill and he helps ETHAN into
> the room. ETHAN has improvised something
> to cover his nakedness.*
>
> *They are both giggling hysterically but trying
> to keep quiet, too*)

MALCOLM

Ssshh, my mother! She'll hear us. Did you see the look on that nun when we ran across the playground?

ETHAN

I think she fainted, Malcolm! I haven't laughed so hard since—! I'm sorry.

> (*MALCOLM claps his hand over ETHAN's
> mouth. Silence. Suddenly the two near-naked
> men become aware of the sexuality of their
> position. Gently, ETHAN takes MALCOLM's
> hand from his mouth. Their faces are close
> together. They stare at each other for a long
> moment, a hair breath away from kissing*)

MALCOLM

Something's wrong.

> (*He goes to door and listens*)

Mom?

> (*He opens door and leaves*)

Mom?

> (**ETHAN** *stands alone, uncertain what to do, when*
> *he hears* **MALCOLM** *call from off*)

Ethan, it's my mother. Come quick!

TRANSITION

> (*A police station.*
>
> **JERRY**, **HAROLD** and **HORSE** are covered
> in blankets. **JEANETTE** is no stranger to a pinch)

JEANETTE
That matron wanted to strip search me. I told her, "You don't want to go there, lady."

HORSE
I think these are your jeans, Jerry.

JERRY
What do you mean I can't see him? He's my son. I haven't been charged with anything.

POLICE SERGEANT
Sorry. He's a minor. The Social Worker wants to talk to him. His mom's coming for him.

> (**PAM** *and* **TEDDY** *arrive at the station*)

PAM
I'm Pam Lukowski. I've come to pick up my son.

POLICE SERGEANT
Just a minute, ma'am.

(*He goes*)

JERRY
Everything's fine, Pam. No one's been charged.

PAM
So this is your great money-making enterprise, Jerry? Pornography?

JERRY
Don't be crazy. I'm trying to get your money for you.

PAM
My money? Nathan's money, don't you mean? I couldn't believe it when they told me at the bank. You almost had me fooled.

(*DUTY SERGEANT* returns with *NATHAN*)

TEDDY
Nathan, are you all right?

NATHAN
I'm fine. Hi, mom.

PAM
Come on, Nathan.

NATHAN
I'm with Dad this weekend.

PAM
Change of plan, darling.

NATHAN
They're taking me away from him, aren't they?

TEDDY

Unemployed, criminal record, child support arrears of close to fifteen hundred dollars, now arrest for indecent exposure. Still think you're a good father, Jerry?

(*JERRY would love to deck him!*)

NATHAN

He's trying. You don't know how hard he's trying.

JERRY

Thanks, honey.

TEDDY

Bit late for that.

NATHAN

I'll be there Sunday, Dad. Somehow.

(*TEDDY and NATHAN leave*)

PAM

Look at yourself, Jerry, just look at yourself.

JERRY

Are you going to marry him?

PAM

Would you blame me?

JERRY

No.

PAM

You said something else on the Maid of the Mist. You said, "Pam, I won't ever let you down." Start with yourself, Jerry. Do something you're proud of. Forget about me and Nath. We're fine. Goodbye, Jerry.

(She goes)

JERRY
What is a man? Why does he bother?
'Cause he's a man, 'cause he's a father.
He wants his kid. He wants his life.

TRANSITION

(A salvation army band is heard piping a
mournful hymn. Over it we can hear a
MINISTER *droning a funereal litany of*
platitudes for the dearly departed. We are
at the small final rites for **MALCOLM'S** *mom.*

The rest of the current Gang is present.
They stand downstage from the other
mourners, at a little distance from **MALCOLM**
and the casket.

DAVE, *apart from them, is wearing his new*
Wal-Mart security guard outfit)

MINISTER
Molly MacGregor was not a great woman, she wasn't a famous one, I'm told a lot of people didn't even like her but she loved her son. God's eye is on a woman such as this as surely as it is on His tiniest sparrow. Let us pray: the Lord is my shepherd, I shall not want. He maketh me to lie down in green pastures. He leadeth me beside still waters. He restoreth my soul. He leadeth me in the paths of righteousness for his name's sake. Yea, though I walk through the valley of the shadow of death, I shall fear no evil for Thou art with me.

(Maybe it's the boredom, maybe it's the
drone of the **MINISTER** *and the hymn but*

somehow the men manage to find a "beat"
in the solemn cadences of the hymn being
sung. Suddenly, **JERRY'S** *hips start moving to*
this private drummer, then **HORSE'S.**
HAROLD *manages a surreptitious twirl.*

DAVE *looks as if he would like to join them.*

They aren't even aware of it at first. But when
they see each other, they can't suppress the giggles)

ETHAN

Come on, guys, you're at a funeral for Christ's sake!

(They settle down)

MINISTER

Malcolm, would you like to say something?

*(**MALCOLM** steps forward)*

SONG: YOU WALK WITH ME

MALCOLM

Is it the wind
Over my shoulder?
Is it the wind that I hear gently whispering?

Are you alone
There in the valley?
No, not alone for you walk, you walk with me.

Is it the wind there over my shoulder?
Is it your voice calling quietly?
Over the hilltop, down in the valley.
Never alone for you walk with me.

When evening falls
And the air gets colder,
When shadows cover the road I am following

Will I be alone there in the darkness?
No, not alone. Not alone.
(And I'll never be…)

>   (**MALCOLM** *falters. The hymn is picked up by*
>   *someone in the congregation. It is* **ETHAN**.)

ETHAN
Never alone. You are walking, you're walking with me.

>   (*He steps forward and joins* **MALCOLM**. *They finish*
>   *the hymn together. By now they are holding hands*)

MALCOLM & ETHAN
Is it the wind there, over my shoulder?
Is it your voice calling quietly?
Over the hilltop, down in the valley.
Never alone for you walk with me.
Over the hilltop, down in the valley.
Never alone for you walk with me.

>   (**DAVE** *has gone over to* **JERRY**)

DAVE
They're holding hands.

JERRY
Good for them, good for them.

DAVE
I don't even hold Georgie's hand and we're married.

MALCOLM
Never alone for you walk with me.

>   (*Light fade on funeral, the last on*
>   **MALCOLM** *and* **ETHAN**)

TRANSITION

> (*JERRY, HAROLD, HORSE and DAVE are
> walking home from the funeral. ESTELLE and
> some girlfriends are approaching from the
> opposite direction*)

JERRY

Gentlemen, meet your audience.

> (*He takes out some tickets*)

Hey Estelle! Hope you got your tickets, ladies. We're nearly clean.

ESTELLE

That's not what we heard. The Bills are playing the same night. Tony Giordano's telling people you're already a bust. Besides, we just had the real thing. Why should we pay good money to see a bunch of amateurs?

HORSE

We're better.

ESTELLE

Than Chippendales? I don't think so, Pop-Pops.

HAROLD

We're different.

ESTELLE

Gentlemen, in that department, you're all pretty much the same. I think I'll go to the game.

JERRY

You'll be sorry. Those Chippendales didn't go all the way. We go all the way, don't we, guys?

HORSE

We what?

ESTELLE

You what?

JERRY

You heard me. What do they call it? The Full Monty. What you ladies wanna see Sunday night is what you're gonna get.

ESTELLE

The Full Monty? You don't have the guts.

JERRY

(*Calling her bluff*)

Don't we?

ESTELLE

I'll take two tickets. I've *seen* the Bills play.

DOLORES

Yeah, but you've also seen Jerry's —

ESTELLE

Shut up!

JERRY

Who's the other ticket for?

ESTELLE

My mother. She needs a good jump-start.

SUSAN

If you're going all the way, I'll take ten.

JOANIE

Do you take Visa?

HORSE

I do now, foxy lady.

*(ESTELLE'S friends are buying tickets, too.
The Gang is seeing actual cash for the first
time in a long while!)*

HAROLD

You never said anything about going all the way.

JERRY

She's right about the tickets. I didn't want to tell you guys. We gotta give 'em something those Chippendales don't.

HAROLD

Yeah, I know: it's called niche marketing, but we're talking about our dicks.

DOLORES

Four, please. You're sexy.

HAROLD

Thank you.

DOLORES

In a non-threatening way.

*(Selling tickets like hotcakes, HAROLD and
HORSE move off. The women are screaming
"The Full Monty, they're going the Full Monty!"
DAVE and JERRY remain)*

JERRY

You look pathetic in that uniform. I almost didn't recognize you at the funeral.

DAVE

Don't rub it in.

JERRY

Your costume's still waiting for you if you want to change your mind about Sunday.

DAVE

I can't, Jer. I promised Georgie I'd give Wal-Mart a try. Don't you think I want to be up there with you and the guys on the big night?

JERRY

What's stopping you? There's a word for men like you and it's not a pretty one.

DAVE

I love my wife.

JERRY

We were supposed to be in this thing together, like we always were. Best friends.

DAVE

We still are.

JERRY

When the chips were down, I always knew you'd end up wimping out at the mall.

DAVE

Go to hell.

JERRY

What do you want me to say, you fat bastard?

(*Something snaps for* DAVE. *He grabs* JERRY *by the shirt*)

DAVE

Don't you ever call me a fat bastard again. Ever. All right? All right?

JERRY

Okay, okay.

DAVE

I better get back to work. I don't want to get fired my first day.

(*He goes, leaving* JERRY *looking after him*)

TERRENCE MCNALLY & DAVID YAZBEK

TRANSITION

(The two REPO MEN cross the stage
with VICKI'S sunbed. VICKI is waiting
for HAROLD when he comes home from
the funeral)

REPO MAN #1

(To HAROLD)
Sorry, mac, it's a job. Somebody's gotta do it.

(They exit with the sunbed)

VICKI

So. The nice man who took the Audi came back with the loose change you'd left in the ashtray. That was nice of him. The people for the sunbed weren't half so accommodating.

HAROLD

I must have been crazy thinking I could keep it from you.

VICKI

How long has it been?

HAROLD

Six months.

VICKI

Out of a job for six months and you didn't tell me? Why, Harold?

HAROLD

I thought something would turn up.

VICKI

I'm your wife, Harold, how do you think that makes me feel? "For better or worse," we said. I meant it, didn't you?

HAROLD

I was afraid you'd leave me if you knew. You like nice things. I want you to have them.

VICKI

Then you don't know me, Harold. Maybe we still don't know each other. I can cope with losing the Audi, the VCR. I can even cope with the neighbors watching our life being repossessed.

(Calling off)

What are you looking at, Mrs. Sullivan!

(Continuing with HAROLD)

Nosy bitch! What I can't cope with is being strangers. We're in this together. I love you, Harold, not what you can buy me. I hated that sunbed. It made us look orange.

TRANSITION

(Early evening. DAVE comes home from his job at Wal-Mart to a dark house)

DAVE

Georgie? Honey?

(GEORGIE is waiting for him with a packed suitcase)

There you are! Not such a bad first day. Beats hanging around the house waiting for you to come home. What's wrong?

GEORGIE

I should have guessed when you started wearing the after-shave. You didn't put it on for me, did you?

DAVE

Georgie...

(She holds up his G-string distastefully)

GEORGIE

But this...I didn't think you were into this sort of thing. It explains a few things at least.

DAVE

It's not what you're thinking, Georgie.

GEORGIE

All those nights coming home late. Stupid cow here thinking you were looking for a job. No wonder. No fucking wonder.

DAVE

I was with Jerry and some guys.

GEORGIE

One of Jerry's little whores, you mean. She'd have to be to be into this sort of...shit.

(She throws the G-string at him)

DAVE

Shut up a minute, will you? It's nothing to do with another woman, all right? I'm...I was a stripper, okay? Me and Jerry and some guys from the factory thought we could pick up some quick cash taking our clothes off like those Chippendales you were so hot for.

GEORGIE

Strippers.

DAVE

All right, all right, I know.

GEORGIE

You and Jerry? Strippers?

DAVE

We weren't that bad.

(He performs a perfect, if lackluster, twirl.
GEORGIE raises her eyebrows, impressed)

I've been practicing for a couple of weeks. Only I couldn't, could I?

GEORGIE
Why not?

DAVE
Because.

GEORGIE
Because what?

DAVE
Well look at me.

GEORGIE
So?

DAVE
Georgie, who wants to see *this* dance?

GEORGIE
Me, Dave. I do.

(She goes to him. She puts her head on his massive stomach and
then wraps her arms around him as VICKI and HAROLD return)

SONG REPRISE: YOU RULE MY WORLD

GEORGIE
I look at you and what I see,
The only man I ever loved in front of me.
I chose you, Dave, it hasn't changed.
You're everything I want, you rule my world.

VICKI

Look at you, you're standing there.
You're still a prince,
You're still the answer to a prayer.
And what I see is all I want.
You're everything.

GEORGIE

You're everything.

VICKI

Anywhere you go, I'll be there.

GEORGIE

Anywhere, I'll follow you.

VICKI

Anything you want I'll give you.

GEORGIE

Anything at all.

VICKI

Anytime you're lost,

VICKI & GEORGIE

That's me there, I'm with you.

VICKI	GEORGIE
I'll see you back home.	*I'll take you home.*

GEORGIE

Look at me.

VICKI

Look at me, Harold.

GEORGIE

And hold me tight.

VICKI

Honey, don't you understand?

GEORGIE

You're like the morning sun to me, but twice as bright.

VICKI

I'll never let you go.

GEORGIE

And what I see is what I get

VICKI & GEORGIE

And it's everything I want.
You rule my world,
My world.

GEORGIE

You're everything I need.

TRANSITION

(Backstage at TONY GIORDANO'S club.
The excitement is palpable. The Gang is in
various states of undress, getting ready to go on.

TONY GIORDANO, the club owner, is
present. He has a big wad of twenty dollar bills)

TONY

I owe you gentlemen an apology. They're lined up around the block. We're gonna have to do a second show.

JERRY

It's supposed to be women only. It's half men, you bastard.

TONY

Nobody told me.

JERRY
Tell 'em to go home. We'll give the money back.

TONY
Look who's getting cold feet!

JERRY
I'm not getting cold feet. We had an agreement.

TONY
Tell close to a thousand horny women there's no show? They'll tear us to pieces.

HAROLD
Ever see a zebra brought down by a pack of wolves, Jerry? Marvelous, those nature films on PBS. Marvelous.

(*KENO comes into the dressing room*)

KENO
It's standing room only out there.

TONY
This is Keno, guys. He's a real stripper.

KENO
We were driving through town and saw the poster.

(*To JERRY*)

I had you figured all wrong. The Full Monty! You're a better man than I am, Gunga Din.

(*He hugs JERRY*)

HAROLD
You're lucky we're only doing this one night or we'd put you guys out of business.

KENO

I'm through after Poughkeepsie. I'm going to be doing the weather for WXXI in Rochester. I'm going to lose my seat. Break a leg.

(*He goes*)

HORSE

My minister's out there.

HAROLD

Jeanette told you not to peek.

HORSE

He's with my mother.

HAROLD

She'll get over it.

HORSE

I'm talking about me!

ETHAN

Can we not talk about mothers? We have someone in mourning here.

MALCOLM

That's okay. This would have killed her anyway.

(*VICKI pops in*)

VICKI

Harold, you left your contacts. Did he tell you his good news? He got a job offer today, a good one.

HAROLD

I asked Vicki if she thought I should still do this. Tell 'em what you told me, honey.

VICKI

I said, "Harold, you have the rest of your life to wear a suit and a tie but only one night to be a member of *Hot Metal*."

(*She goes*)

HAROLD

Shall we do a warm-up?

JERRY

We have to wait for Dave.

HAROLD

We've been through this: Dave's not coming.

JERRY

Everything we rehearsed was for the six of us. I'm not going out there unless we're a team.

(*DAVE enters*)

DAVE

There was nothing on television, so I said to Georgie, what the hell? I might as well go the Full Monty with the fellas.

(*They surround DAVE with hugs and cheers.
JERRY stays where he is*)

HORSE

What's your excuse now, Jerry?

HAROLD

He doesn't have one.

DAVE

Gentlemen, give me wide berth. I am on fire.

(*He demonstrates what is in store for their audience.
GEORGIE enters with NATHAN in tow*)

GEORGIE
Found this one in the parking lot.

NATHAN
They wouldn't let me in.

JERRY
What are you doing here? Your mother will have a fit.

NATHAN
She's in the third row.

JERRY
Did she bring Teddy with her?

NATHAN
Yeah, and he brought his binoculars.

*(JEANETTE pops into the dressing room.
She is glammed-up for the occasion)*

JEANETTE
Okay, fellas, they're calling places.

HAROLD
Thanks, Jeanette. We couldn't have done it without you.

JEANETTE
It's going to be hard going back to that rocking chair after this. I called my agent to tell him I was thinking of getting back in the business. They said he died ten years ago. "A dead agent," I said, "that's definitely an oxymoron." Good luck, boys. Come on.

(She takes GEORGIE and NATHAN in tow)

HAROLD
This is it.

MALCOLM
Should we get in a circle and pray?

HORSE
Malcolm!

MALCOLM
That's what the Bills do.

HORSE
I'm trying to stay focused.

(With the exception of JERRY, the Gang lines up to go on)

ETHAN
Guys, when I get nervous there's a lot less glimmer.

HORSE
(Fatherly advice)
Happens to the best of us, Ethan.

MALCOLM
You'll be fine, Eth. Let's go!

(HAROLD, ETHAN & MALCOLM go)

HORSE
Lord, thank you for taking this burden from me and giving it to
that poor white boy!

(He goes)

DAVE
Here we are again, ol' buddy. Edge of the cliff, ready to jump.
Butch Cassidy and...what's the matter?

JERRY
I can't do it. I can't go out there.

DAVE

What are you talking about? This was your idea.

JERRY

They're gonna be laughing at us.

DAVE

I don't blame them. It's going to be pretty funny.

JERRY

Not to me it won't. They're expecting Jerry Lukowski!

DAVE

Well give 'em Jerry Lukowski.

JERRY

Let a thousand strangers look at me without my clothes on?

(*The Gang returns*)

DAVE

I believe that's the general idea in a strip club.

HAROLD

Guys, it's places! You're either in or you're out, Lukowski.

JERRY

I'm out.

(*He starts to change into his street clothes*)

HORSE

If he's not going out there with us, I'm not going the Full Monty.

MALCOLM

Neither am I.

TERRENCE MCNALLY & DAVID YAZBEK

ETHAN

I don't mind. I'll go the Full Monty.

HORSE

Who asked you, Godzilla!

DAVE

(Taking charge now)

No, one of us doesn't go the Full Monty, none of us does. We'll give 'em a good show and leave the rest to their imagination.

(The others charge out, eager to perform)

DAVE

So long, Jerry.

(He goes as JERRY continues changing. We can hear the music and the women off)

TRANSITION

(The stage of TONY GIORDANO'S club, as in the first scene. Fanfare from the band. Pandemonium at the sight of JEANETTE. She motions for silence)

JEANETTE

Ladies and gentlemen. I'm afraid I have bad news.

(Groans from the audience)

I'm not going to be taking my clothes off tonight. But somebody is! They may not be young, they may not be pretty and they may not be very good but for one night and one night only, they're here, they're live and they're going for no less than the Full Monty.

(*JEANETTE tears into the opening music.
Band up at once.*

The five men enter and begin to dance)

SONG: LET IT GO

ETHAN
*Did I capture your imagination?
Did I break you down and make you smile?
It's a serious little situation.
Why don't we loosen up and dance awhile?*

DAVE
You need a loose-lipped lover with a heart of honey.

HAROLD
You need a sex cadet when duty calls.

MALCOLM
Come on show me all your bare-faced beauty.

HORSE
I wanna see our shadows bouncing off the walls.

ETHAN, MALCOLM, DAVE, HORSE & HAROLD
*Let it go, let it go. Loosen up, yeah, let it go.
Let it go, let it go. It's all right.
Let it go, let it go. Shake it up now, let it go.
You just tell me when you think you're ready.*

GEORGIE
(*From the audience*)
Hey *Hot Metal*, where's the rest of you? I paid for six hunks.
Excuse me, I'm counting five.

Yeah, let's see it, Harold. I brought my telescope!

I'll tell you what you can do with that telescope.

REG
Who are you, lady?

VICKI
I'm his wife!

TRANSITION

> (*Backstage.* **JERRY** *hasn't moved. We can hear the music and the* *women off.* **NATHAN** *comes into the room*)

NATHAN
Dad, what are you doing?

JERRY
They're getting their show. Nobody's gonna miss me.

NATHAN
You gotta go out there. You gave the guys your word.

JERRY
They know better than to listen to me.

NATHAN
You gave me your word.

JERRY
Don't worry, I'll get you your money back.

NATHAN

I'm not talking about the money. I'm talking about you.

JERRY

Don't get all grown up on me.

NATHAN

Dad, just this once, no wise cracks.

JERRY

Okay, Nath, what is it?

NATHAN

This time, don't be what everyone thinks you are, a loser.

JERRY

Who are you calling a loser?

NATHAN

You're my father. You're almost a great father. You said you needed to make a killing. This is it. Everybody we know is out there.
Show 'em.

JERRY

You think I'm a great father?

NATHAN

I said almost. I love you, you big fuck.

> (He cuffs JERRY. This time JERRY doesn't
> cuff him back. NATHAN leaves)

TRANSITION

> (The five men are dancing on stage to the
> cheers of the audience)

TERRENCE McNALLY & DAVID YAZBEK

MALCOLM
Just let the music be the master.

HORSE
I got a whammy bar on my brown guitar.

ETHAN & HAROLD
You can play me like a stratocaster.

(The roar goes up as JERRY takes his place on stage in the line. With such an incredible response from their audience, the six men are transformed into something Chippendale's would be proud of. That is, what they lack in technique, they more than make up for in their rapport with the crowd. These guys are charisma personified)

JERRY
'Cause here I am—and baby, there you are.

ETHAN & JERRY
Well I'm a rocket boy with a touch like silver.

HORSE & HAROLD
And I'm crashing through your bedroom door.

MALCOLM, JERRY & ETHAN
And I'm ready like I hope you're ready.

JERRY
Come on, I'll show you mine if you show me yours!

(At one point, GEORGIE can't restrain herself any longer. She runs up from the audience and onto the stage and gives DAVE a big hug and kiss. She pantomimes to audience "He's mine!" She runs back to her seat)

MEN

Let it go. Let it go. Loosen up, yeah let it go.
Let it go, let it go, it's all right.

Let it go. Let it go. Shake it up now, let it go.
You just tell me when you think you're ready.

Let it go. Let it go. Loosen up, yeah let it go.
Let it go, let it go, it's all right.
Let it go. Let it go. Shake it up now, let it go.

MEN

Let it go —

> (*Pretty soon the men are down to their
> boxers. They strike a final pose.*
>
> *This is met by boos and a tepid response
> from the audience*)

JOANIE

We were promised the Full Monty! The poster said the Full Monty!

GEORGIE

Hey, what about it, Davie! I don't mind!

VICKI

Take it off, Harold, take it all off!

PAM

You heard her, Jerry. Let's go.

TEDDY

Hey, Lukowski, I dare you! You're not man enough!

TERRENCE MCNALLY & DAVID YAZBEK

ESTELLE

(*Waving a bill*)
I got twenty that says you won't do it Jerry.

PAM

(*Waving a bill*)
I got fifty that says he will.

(*Stirring the audience*)

Hey, hey, whadda 'ya say. Buffalo men go all the way!

WOMEN

Hey, hey, whadda 'ya say. Buffalo men go all the way!
Hey, hey, whadda 'ya say. Buffalo men go all the way!

(**GEORGIE, VICKI** *and* **OTHER WOMEN**
encourage the audience to pick up the chant.
This could get out of hand.

The audience is demanding its Full Monty!

The men, all at sea, look to **JERRY** *for what to do now*)

JERRY

Gentlemen, we only live once!

MEN

Let it go. Let it go.
Loosen up, yeah let it go.
Let it go, let it go, it's all right.

Let it go. Let it go.
Shake it up now, let it go.
You just tell me when you think you're ready.

JERRY

Are you ready?

MEN	WOMEN
Let it go. Let it go.	*Let it go. Let it go.*
Loosen up, yeah let it go.	*Let it go, go.*
Let it go, let it go, it's all right.	*Let it go. Let it go.*
	Let it go, go.
Let it go. Let it go.	*Let it go. Let it go.*
Shake it up now, let it go.	*Let it go, go.*
Let it go —	

> *(The men resume dancing. This time when the moment of truth comes, they do not shirk from it. They turn their backs to us and drop their G-strings.*
>
> *The audience is going crazy.*
>
> *The men turn around. They are grinning from ear to ear.*
>
> *Black out)*

THE END